BIO: Jeffery A Carlson

Was born in 1946 making me a baby boomer.
Grew up is Minneapolis Area and live here now.

After getting out of HS the Vietnam War called and I joined the Air Force and spent 1965 to 1970 in the Air Force. While in Air Force was trained in a new field called Computers.

Because of the 45th anniversary for my HS, I got involved with Face book. Started writing what I called the Quote of the Day. I could see that many people in the country had no clue how our government works.

So my Quotes of the Day were based on giving education.
That education was for those reading them and of course a learning tool for me.

Many suggested that I write a book using the Quotes of the Day I was producing and with lots of encouragement from a dying mom, I wrote The Party of Scrooge – The history of American Politics.

The book has many quotes and fun facts about Politics both historical and current. Many of the Issues we face are spelled out in the book and can be referenced over and over.

Scrooge, sketched image used for cover of the book was done by myself.

Chapter 1:   Pages 7 - 21
The Party of Scrooge - The History of American Politics:
  My Generation – page 11
  Declaration of Independence – page 13
  United States Constitution – page 16

Chapter 2:   Pages 22 - 41
The Commons:
  Commons definition – page 23
  First Five Presidents – the Founding Fathers
    George Washington – page 25
    John Adams – page 26
    Thomas Jefferson – page 28
      Tyranny by Jeff Carlson – page 30
    James Madison – page 31
    James Monroe – page 33
  Education mainstay of the Commons – page 35
  Water Control under attack – page 39

Chapter 3:   Pages 42 - 73
Know your enemy because they are right here in America and Hiding in plain sight
  Who did this Accountability 2000 – 2006 – page 42
  Fear and the Patriot Act – page 43
  American Dream by Jeff Carlson – page 45
  Austerity – page 47
  Filibuster – page 48
  The Ryan Bill and Vision for America – page 55
  Alec, Chamber of Commerce and Wall Street – page 59
  Twenty Most dangerous men – page 63

Chapter 4:   Pages 74 - 97
President Barack Obama
  His accomplishments a list that is still growing – page 75
  Affordable Care Act – page 93

Chapter 5:   Pages 98 - 137
Review the Issues Facing the Country
    Supreme Court – page 98
    Medicare – page 99
    Social Security – page 101
    Education – page 102
    EPA – page 107
    FDA – page 109
        Monsanto – page 110
        Killing Bees – page 111
    War never ending – page 113
    Labor – page 118
    When they came for me: Martin Niemöller – page 120
    Voting Rights – page 121
    Women's Rights – page 122
    Immigration – page 122
    Grover Norquist – page 125
    Student Loans and lets fix it – page 126
    Dare to call it Treason – page 129

Chapter 6:   Pages 138 - 184
Information you need to know
    Civics 101 – page 138
    Economics 101 – page 139
    Electoral College – page 144
    History of American Corporations – page 147
    Unions – page 150
    Fascism 14 steps – page 172
    The Small Business – page 182
        Ode to the pizza man – page 183

Chapter 7:   Pages 185 - 209
Moving Forward
    Abe Lincoln – page 185
    Bill Clinton – page 186
    President Barrack Obama – page 194
    America at a Crossroads – page 204
    Crossroads my Vision – page 206

Chapter 8:   Pages 210 - 211
Epilogue – page 210

The Party of Scrooge
History of American Politics

Written by Jeffery A. Carlson

Scrooge Image drawing by Jeffery A. Carlson

THE PARTY OF SCROOGE
THE HISTORY OF AMERICAN POLITICS

I would like to dedicate this book to my Mother Geraldine Carlson, who encouraged me to write this book to the day she died 01/07/2012.

My mom was all about being Liberal and standing up for all those who could not stand up for themselves.

In this book I hope to show you that through Quotes and History how things do not change unless we use History as a guide to making the changes that benefit us all.

> **"History is the window to all that humans have accomplished, history is also the window to all that humans need to accomplish"**
> Jeff Carlson

I would also like to give a shout out to all those in Wisconsin who have fought so hard to rid themselves of a very evil man in Scott Walker.

It was Wisconsin that got me going on my Quotes of the Day. I could not believe that the Media was not reporting what was going on and when they did they reported only the Right Wing view.

The Wisconsin results, came in and Citizen United won over People Power. Walker outspent Barrett 7 to 1 and the lies and money won out.

Here is a quote I wrote that fits my Mood about that:

"Wisconsin gave us a good right punch to the mouth, we spit out a few teeth and blood flows, we get mean and come back fighting with more determination than ever to stop fascism in America."
Jeff Carlson

Why Scrooge that is a question that has been asked of me more than once. I started calling the GOP Scrooge when they were going all out to Blackmail the American People and OBAMA into extending the BUSH TAX cuts back in November 2010.

What we got for that blackmail was millions of Americans were able to keep their Unemployment coming in and Don't Ask Don't Tell was repealed.

Then in March of 2011, I read about how the GOP was passing laws to put people in jail if they could not pay their bills and the states were using the Unemployment list to go after people in trouble. Private Prisons needed to be filled and the GOP were more than willing to help.

"From this day forward the GOP will be 'Scrooge the Ugly One'. Until the Ghosts of Compassion, Honesty, and Brotherhood comes to visit and take them back to being human, they will remain Scrooge".
Jeff Carlson

Lets start with a little Charles Dickens, A Christmas Carol: The Good.

"But I am sure that I have always thought of Christmas time, when it has come round... as a good time; a kind, forgiving, charitable, pleasant time; the only time I know of, in the long calendar of the year, when men and women seem by one consent to open their shut-up hearts freely."

"I will honor Christmas in my heart, and try to keep it all the year."

Charles Dickens, A Christmas Carol: The Old Ugly Greedy Scrooge.

"At this festive season of the year, Mr. Scrooge," said the gentleman, taking up a pen, "it is more than usually desirable that we should make some slight provision for the Poor and Destitute, who suffer greatly at the present time. Many thousands are in want of common necessaries; hundreds of thousands are in want of common comforts, sir."

"Are there no prisons?" asked Scrooge.

"Plenty of prisons," said the gentleman, laying down the pen again.

"And the Union workhouses?" demanded Scrooge. "Are they still in operation?"

"They are. Still," returned the gentleman, "I wish I could say they were not."

"The Treadmill and the Poor Law are in full vigour, then?" said Scrooge.

"Both very busy, sir."

"Oh! I was afraid, from what you said at first, that something had occurred to stop them in their useful course," said Scrooge. "I'm very glad to hear it."

"Under the impression that they scarcely furnish Christian cheer of mind or body to the multitude," returned the gentleman, "a few of us are endeavouring to raise a fund to buy the Poor some meat and drink and means of warmth. We choose this time, because it is a time, of all others, when Want is keenly felt, and Abundance rejoices. What shall I put you down for?"

"Nothing!" Scrooge replied.

"You wish to be anonymous?"

"I wish to be left alone," said Scrooge. "Since you ask me what I wish, gentlemen, that is my answer. I don't make merry myself at Christmas and I can't afford to make idle people merry. I help to support the establishments I have mentioned -- they cost enough; and those who are badly off must go there."

"Many can't go there; and many would rather die."

"If they would rather die," said Scrooge, "they had better do it, and decrease the surplus population. Besides -- excuse me -- I don't know that."

"But you might know it," observed the gentleman.

"It's not my business," Scrooge returned. "It's enough for a man to understand his own business, and not to interfere with other people's. Mine occupies me constantly. Good afternoon, gentlemen!"

Seeing clearly that it would be useless to pursue their point, the gentlemen withdrew. Scrooge returned his labours with an improved opinion of himself, and in a more facetious temper than was usual with him.

Scrooge lives on in the Form of the current GOP.

What you see coming from the GOP in this country is a total lack of compassion for those that have been hit by the policies of the GOP. In fact they like to blame the victims of the Bush Recession, so that they can justify cutting unemployment and safety nets put in place to give dignity to those in need. Now does that not sound like Mr. Scrooge.

Again in October 2011, the news was the Post Office is failing and I was wondering what happened. Turns out in recess session the GOP past a poison pill bill that was to do one thing and that was to destroy the Post Office and end the 700,000 Union Jobs that made up the Post Office. The bill required the Post Office to pay for all retirement benefits for 75 years all this to be done to in a 10-year time frame. No Company has ever been forced to this and it cannot be done without bankrupting the Company, exactly what the GOP was looking for. By the Way the Democrats have been trying to repair the damage ever since and have been blocked by the GOP.

Here is a Rant Quote I put out after I had found out about what the GOP had done to the Post Office.

Quote of the Day   By Jeff Carlson

"A party that held the Unemployed hostage to get Tax breaks for only the Rich
A Party that held the country hostage and destroyed our credit rating
A Party that that deliberately sabotaged a American Icon the Post Office
A Party that wants to end all the safety nets that would devastate seniors
A Party that had a chance to create 1 million Jobs and would not

This Party uses Lies, Fear and Hate to pull in its base
This Party hides behind religion yet has no morals
This Party needs to be called out
This Party needs to be run out of Office
This Party is called The Party of Scrooge."

MY GENERATION

I was born in 1946 and I am a Baby Boomer. We were the Hippies, rock and roll and we will change the world. We listen to JFK and joined the Peace Corps, we saw man walk on the Moon the world was ours to make better.

"My fellow Americans, ask not what your country can do for you, ask what you can do for your country."
John F. Kennedy

"Human progress is neither automatic nor inevitable... Every step toward the goal of justice requires sacrifice, suffering, and struggle; the tireless exertions and passionate concern of dedicated individuals"
Martin Luther King, Jr.

"Few will have the greatness to bend history itself; but each of us can work to change a small portion of events, and in the total; of all those acts will be written the history of this generation."
Robert Kennedy

John F. Kennedy, Martin Luther King, Jr. and Robert Kennedy, died so that we would have a better country and now the Right Wing extremist want to end everything they stood for.

Makes this election is so important because what they stood for is what makes America the envy of the World.

My generation, where are we taking this country?

My parent's generation was called the "Greatest":

They gave us so many things:
**They fought to give us unions: --- 40 hour work week --- Benefits --- Vacations --- Safety at the work place and many, many other wonderful things that improve the quality of our worker's and family's lives.
**They gave us women's rights that gave women the right to vote.
**They ended children being exploited in the work force.
**They gave us an education system better than any in the world.
**They fought a war that kept the world free.
**They gave us Social Security.
**They gave us Medicare and many safety nets.
**They gave us Civil Rights.

**They gave us the science and technology to go to the moon.
**They gave us technology for the Internet and Freedom to express ourselves.
**They gave us laws to protect the air and the water.

My Generation, the Baby Boomers will be called "The Greediest Generation".

We have a party called the Republicans that is run by people from My Generation. Add in a mixture of the GEN X (the me generation) names you might know are Paul Ryan, Eric Cantor, Rand Paul and the one and only Sarah Palin.

Note about the Gen X generation is that for at least the republicans they believe in I got mine and the hell with you via (Ayn Rand).
Paul Ryan budget is all about just that, another word for it is Austerity.

**They want to control women at every level from jobs to contraception
**They want to destroy the unions.
**They want to suppress as many voters and they can.
**They want to end child labor laws and again exploit children.
**They want to end the Public Education System.
**They want to start a WAR in IRAN after they started an illegal war in IRAQ
**They want to Privatize Social Security
**They want to destroy Medicare and all the Safety Nets.
**They want to roll back Civil Rights.
**They want to end real Science and use right wing ideology
**They want to end the freedom of the Internet.
**They want to end the EPA and protection of the Air and water.

Please help me in 2012 and save my Generation from themselves by Voting Democratic.

Many times I have heard that there is no difference in the parties to this I came up with this Quote:

"When we encounter those that say there is no difference in the Parties, one simply puts that nothing that the Democrats support hurts or tries to control people, everything that the GOP supports hurts or tries to control people"
Jeff Carlson

Lets take some time and learn about where we came from before we figure out where we need to go.

Declaration of Independence

From Wikipedia, the free encyclopedia

56 delegates to the Continental Congress Purpose To announce and explain separation from Great Britain.

The Declaration of Independence was a statement adopted by the Continental Congress on July 4, 1776, which announced that the thirteen American colonies, then at war with Great Britain, regarded themselves as independent states, and no longer a part of the British Empire.

John Adams put forth a resolution earlier in the year which made a formal declaration inevitable.

A committee was assembled to draft the formal declaration, to be ready when congress voted on independence. Adams persuaded the committee to select Thomas Jefferson to compose the original draft of the document, which congress would edit to produce the final version.

The Declaration was ultimately a formal explanation of why Congress had voted on July 2 to declare independence from Great Britain, more than a year after the outbreak of the American Revolutionary War.

The Independence Day of the United States of America is celebrated on July 4, the day Congress approved the wording of the Declaration.

Have you ever wondered what happened to the 56 men who signed the Declaration of Independence?

Five signers were captured by the British as traitors, and tortured before they died. Twelve had their homes ransacked and burned. Two lost their sons serving in the Revolutionary Army; another had two sons captured. Nine of the 56 fought and died from wounds or hardships of the Revolutionary War. They signed and they pledged their lives, their fortunes, and their sacred honor. What kind of men were they?

Twenty-four were lawyers and jurists. Eleven were merchants, nine were farmers and large plantation owners; men of means, well educated. But they signed the Declaration of Independence knowing full well that the penalty would be death if they were captured.

Quotes on the Declaration of Independence:

I will start this with a quote from the first president of this great country:

"As Mankind becomes more liberal, they will be more apt to allow that all those who conduct themselves as worthy members of the community are equally entitled to the protections of civil government. I hope ever to see America among the foremost nations of justice and liberality."
George Washington (1st US President (1789-97))

Washington really was saying we must work together as a nation and make sure all the people of this country have the opportunity to live with dignity.

"We hold these truths to be self-evident, that all men are created equal, that they are endowed by their Creator with certain unalienable Rights, that among these are Life, Liberty and the pursuit of Happiness."
Thomas Jefferson (1743-1826)

Note in this quote it has often said Jefferson was talking about the "Right to Privacy", but he used the words Pursuit of Happiness, why you ask, because at that time the "Right to Privacy", was what was said when one wanted to use the bathroom.

The Right Wing often claims there is no Right to Privacy in the Constitution.

"They that can give up essential liberty to obtain a little temporary safety deserve neither liberty nor safety."
Benjamin Franklin (1706-1790)

The GOP uses fear as one of their tools to control their base. We got the Patriot Act because of FEAR.

"I always consider the settlement of America with reverence and wonder, as the opening of a grand scene and design in providence, for the illumination of the ignorant and the emancipation of the slavish part of mankind all over the earth."
John Adams (1735-1826)

"I am well aware of the toil and blood and treasure it will cost us to maintain this declaration, and support and defend these states. Yet through all the gloom I see the rays of ravishing light and glory. I can see that the end is worth all the means. This is our day of deliverance."
John Adams (1735-1826)

"That these united colonies are, and of right ought to be, free and independent states; that they are absolved from all allegiance to the British crown; and that all political connection between them and the State of Great Britain is, and ought to be, totally dissolved."
Richard Henry Lee (1732-1794)

"There, I guess King George will be able to read that."
John Hancock (1737-1793)

"Equal and exact justice to all men...freedom of religion, freedom of the press, freedom of person under the protection of the habeas corpus; and trial by juries impartially selected, these principles form the bright constellation which has gone before us."
Thomas Jefferson (1743-1826)

All these freedoms that Jefferson talks about are under attack mainly from the Right but many of the Left have joined in and are working for the Corporations to undermine the Freedoms we have always enjoyed.

Here are some quotes that I put together about the Revolutions then and Now.

"Those who make peaceful revolutions impossible will make violent revolutions inevitable"
John Fitzgerald Kennedy (American 35th US President (1961-63), 1917-1963)

"Poverty is the parent of revolution"
Aristotle (Ancient Greek Philosopher, Scientist and Physician, 384 BC-322 BC)

"The Framers [of the Constitution] knew that free speech is the friend of change and revolution. But they also knew that it is always the deadliest enemy of tyranny."
Hugo Black (American Jurist, Lawyer and Politician 1886-1971)

John Adams famously told us that the real American Revolution was not the war for independence... he said:
"The Revolution was effected before the War commenced. The Revolution was in the minds and hearts of the people; a change in their religious sentiments of their duties and obligations. This radical change in the principles, opinions, sentiments, and affections of the people, was the real American Revolution."

Here is a quote from me that I think reflects what is going on in America today:

"We are in the mist of a Revolution it may be non-violent or it may get ugly but after thirty years of the Right Wing tearing down and destroying the Middle Class in this country, the people are fed up and saying enough is enough."
Jeff Carlson

We should know something about the Constitution because those on the right are always saying they are the only ones that follow it. Note a huge Lie and they really need to be called out on it each time they open their mouths. There are many complexities in our Constitution and it been changed to meet the growing of a Democracy now under attack from Right Wing ideologies to limit the freedoms all Americans have enjoyed over the last 40 to 70 years depending on race.

United States Constitution

From Wikipedia, the free encyclopedia

The Constitution of the United States is the supreme law of the United States of America.

The first three Articles of the Constitution establish the rules and separate powers of the three branches of the federal government: a legislature, the bicameral Congress; an executive branch led by the President; and a federal judiciary headed by the Supreme
Court. The last four Articles frame the principle of federalism. The Tenth Amendment confirms its federal characteristics.

The Constitution was adopted on September 17, 1787, by the Constitutional Convention in Philadelphia, Pennsylvania, and ratified by conventions in eleven states. It went into effect on March 4, 1789[1]. The first ten constitutional amendments ratified by three-fourths of the states in 1791 are known as the Bill of Rights. The Constitution has been amended seventeen times (for a total of 27 amendments) and its principles are applied in courts of law by judicial review.

The Constitution guides American society in law and political culture. It is the oldest charter of supreme law in continuous use, and it influenced later international figures establishing national constitutions. Recent impulses for reform center on concerns for extending democracy and balancing the federal budget

The Constitution is often hailed as a marvel of brevity and of clarity. It was, however, written in the 18th century, and many of the ideas, concepts, words, phrases, and euphemisms seem odd to us today, if not down right foreign.

Preamble to the United States Constitution

"We the People of the United States, in Order to form a more perfect Union, establish Justice, insure domestic Tranquility, provide for the common defense, promote the general Welfare, and secure the Blessings of Liberty to ourselves and our Posterity, do ordain and establish this Constitution for the United States of America."

The Amendments:
From usconstitution.net

The first ten amendments to the Constitution were all adopted at the same time and are collectively known as the Bill of Rights.

The United States Bill of Rights consists of the ten amendments added to the Constitution in 1791, as supporters of the Constitution had promised critics during the debates of 1788.

The English Bill of Rights (1689) was an inspiration for the American Bill of Rights.

Both required jury trials contain a right to keep and bear arms, prohibit excessive bail and forbid "cruel and unusual punishments." Many liberties protected by state constitutions and the Virginia Declaration of Rights were incorporated into the Bill of Rights.

The 1st Amendment protects the people's right to practice religion, to speak freely, to assemble (meet), to address (petition) the government, and of the press to publish.

The 2nd Amendment protects the right to own guns. There is debate whether this is a right that protects the state, or a right that protects individuals.

The 3rd Amendment guarantees that the army cannot force homeowners to give them room and board.

The 4th Amendment protects the people from the government improperly taking property, papers, or people, without a valid warrant based on probable cause (good reason).

The 5th Amendment protects people from being held for committing a crime unless they are properly indicted, that they may not be tried twice for the same crime, that you need not be forced to testify against yourself, and from property being taken without just compensation. It also contains due process guarantees.

The 6th Amendment guarantees a speedy trial, an impartial jury, that the accused can confront witnesses against them, and that the accused must be allowed to have a lawyer.

The 7th Amendment guarantees a jury trial in federal civil court cases. This type of case is normally no longer heard in federal court.

The 8th Amendment guarantees that punishments will be fair, and not cruel, and that extraordinarily large fines will not be set.

The 9th Amendment is simply a statement that other rights aside from those listed may exist, and just because they are not listed doesn't mean they can be violated.

The 10th Amendment is the subject of some debate, but essentially it states that any power not granted to the federal government belongs to the states or to the people. See the Federalism Topic Page for more information.

The 11th Amendment more clearly defines the original jurisdiction of the Supreme Court concerning a suit brought against a state by a citizen of another state.

The 12th Amendment redefines how the President and Vice-President are chosen by the Electoral College, making the two positions cooperative, rather than first and second highest vote-getters. It also ensures that anyone who becomes Vice-President must be eligible to become President.

The 13th Amendment abolished slavery in the entire United States.

The 14th Amendment ensured that all citizens of all states enjoyed not only rights on the federal level, but on the state level, too. It removed the three-fifths counting of slaves in the census. It ensured that the United States would not pay the debts of rebellious states. It also had several measures designed to ensure the loyalty of legislators who participated on the Confederate side of the Civil War.

The 15th Amendment ensures that race cannot be used as a criteria for voting.

The 16th Amendment authorizes the United States to collect income tax without regard to the population of the states.

The 17th Amendment shifted the choosing of Senators from the state legislatures to the people of the states.

The 18th Amendment abolished the sale or manufacture of alcohol in the United States. This amendment was later repealed (erased).

The 19th Amendment ensures that gender cannot be used as a criteria for voting.

The 20th Amendment set new start dates for the terms of the Congress and the President, and clarifies how the deaths of Presidents before swearing-in would be handled.

The 21st Amendment repealed the 18th Amendment.

The 22nd Amendment set a limit on the number of times a President could be elected - two four-year terms. It has one exception for a Vice-President who assumes the Presidency after the death or removal of the President, establishing the maximum term of any President to 10 years.

The 23rd Amendment grants the District of Columbia (Washington D.C.) the right to three electors in Presidential elections.

The 24th Amendment ensured that no tax could be charged to vote for any federal office.

The 25th Amendment clarifies even further the line of succession to the Presidency, and establishes rules for a President who becomes unable to perform his duties while in office.

The 26th Amendment ensures that any person 18 or over may vote.

The 27th Amendment requires that any law that increased the pay of legislators may not take effect until after an election.

There is much to learned about our constitution but for now here are some Quotes from our founding fathers on the document and country they created for all of us.

Religion and Corporations is what the Founding fathers feared most: Here are some quotes about religion:

"The United States of America should have a foundation free from the influence of clergy."
George Washington, First President of USA

"As the Government of the United States of America is not, in any sense, founded on the Christian religion; as it has in itself no character of enmity against the laws, religion, or tranquillity, of Mussulmen; and, as the said States never entered into any war, or act of hostility against any Mahometan nation, it is declared by the parties, that no pretext arising from religious opinions, shall ever produce an interruption of the harmony existing between the two countries."
~ Tripoli of Barbary. Art. 11. – Authored by American diplomat Joel Barlow in 1796, the following treaty was sent to the floor of the Senate, June 7, 1797, where it was read aloud in its entirety and unanimously approved. John Adams, having seen the treaty, signed it and proudly proclaimed it to the Nation.
John Adams, Second President of the USA

"Millions of innocent men, women and children, since the introduction of Christianity, have been burnt, tortured, fined, imprisoned; yet we have not advanced one inch towards uniformity. What has been the effect of coercion? To make half the world fools, and the other half hypocrites." ,..., "The Christian god is a three-headed monster, cruel, vengeful and capricious. If one wishes to know more of this raging, three-headed beast-like god, one only needs to look at the caliber of people who say they serve him. They are always of two classes: fools and hypocrites.",...,
 "The day will come when the mystical generation of Jesus, by the supreme being as his father in the womb of a virgin, will be classed with the fable of the generation of Minerva in the brain of Jupiter." ~ Thomas Jefferson wrote, in a letter to John Adams (April 11, 1823)
Thomas Jefferson, Third President of the USA:

"The purpose of separation of church and state is to keep forever from these shores the ceaseless strife that has soaked the soil of Europe in blood for centuries."
James Madison, Fourth President of the United States:

Quotes about where we want to be going:

"(T)he foundation of our national policy will be laid in the pure and immutable principles of private morality; ...the propitious smiles of Heaven can never be expected on a nation that disregards the eternal rules of order and right which Heaven itself has ordained..."
George Washington, First Inaugural, April 30 1789

"A wise and frugal government, which shall restrain men from injuring one another, which shall leave them otherwise free to regulate their own pursuits of industry and improvement, and shall not take from the mouth of labor the bread it has earned. This is the sum of good government, and this is necessary to close the circle of our felicity."
Thomas Jefferson, First Inaugural Address.

"The Constitution is not an instrument for the government to restrain the people, it is an instrument for the people to restrain the government."
Patrick Henry

"We base all our experiments on the capacity of mankind for self-government."
James Madison

"I believe that banking institutions are more dangerous to our liberties than standing armies. Already they have raised up a moneyed aristocracy that has set the government at defiance. The issuing power should be taken from the banks and restored to the people, to whom it properly belongs."
Thomas Jefferson

"If the American people ever allow private banks to control the issue of currency, first by inflation, then by deflation, the banks and corporations that will grow up around them will deprive the people of all property until their children wake up homeless on the continent their fathers conquered."
Thomas Jefferson

These last two quotes from Jefferson and there are others from the other Founding Fathers that support what Jefferson is saying. They are the most important because this is where we stand now and a vote for the GOP is a Vote for all that Jefferson warned us against.

Think about that.

"I love History, because you can see the greatest of our leaders understood that the real power in America, is not how much we can accumulate but in the people and the opportunity to better yourself."

Jeff Carlson

The Commons

The Commons is what the founding fathers wanted this country to be built around.

"American Democracy was founded on the Commons, 'What is good for the Commons is good for all', when the Commons is abandoned or attacked, Democracy will be lost"
Jeff Carlson

"We have to be careful not to succumb to this nonsense that a public system is inherently flawed and that therefore we have to turn to the marketplace for solutions. I've never in my entire life seen any evidence that the competitive free market, unrestricted, without a strong counterpoise within the public sector, will ever dispense decent medical care, sanitation, transportation, or education to the people. It's as simple as that."
--Jonathan Kozol, author of "Savage Inequalities" and "Amazing Grace."

Currently the Commons are under attack from the Right in this Country and we the people need to make sure they stay the Commons.

In every state where the GOP has taken power the first thing they do is go after what has always been the Commons. We are talking the Air we breathe, the Water we drink, Schools, Libraries, Roads, Utilities, Police, and Fireman and in many case the Parks.

Think about a America where you have corporations polluting the air and water, no public schools, no libraries, no free parks, no police and fire protection unless you pay a private firm to protect you. You will still be paying taxes but you now will have to pay extra fees, to get what is now the commons and paid for by Federal, State, Local and Property taxes.

This is the vision that the GOP has for America. In Michigan they are homing their skills on how to privatize the Commons and ending the control of the local communities and replacing elected officials with dictators that have the right to take over and sell off all the community properties to private enterprises.

Thomas Jefferson, a relentless critic of the monopolizing of economic power by banks, corporations and those who put their faith in what the third president referred to as:
 "The selfish spirit of commerce (that) knows no country, and feels no passion or principle but that of gain"

"The end of democracy and the defeat of the American Revolution will occur when government falls into the hands of lending institutions and moneyed incorporations."
Thomas Jefferson 1816

You can see that Jefferson would be horrified if he saw the current state of Politics with the Republican Party controlled by moneyed incorporations.

"Information is the currency of democracy."
Thomas Jefferson

THE COMMONS as defined in Wikipedia:

The commons were traditionally defined as the elements of the environment - forests, atmosphere, rivers, fisheries or grazing land - that are shared, used and enjoyed by all.

Today, the commons are also understood within a cultural sphere. These commons include literature, music, arts, design, film, video, television, radio, information, software and sites of heritage.

The commons can also include public goods such as public space, public education, health and the infrastructure that allows our society to function (such as electricity or water delivery systems). There also exists the 'life commons', e.g. the human genome.

Peter Barnes describes commons as a set of assets that have two characteristics: they are all gifts, and they are all shared. A shared gift is one we receive as members of a community, as opposed to individually. Examples of such gifts include air, water, ecosystems, languages, music, holidays, money, law, mathematics, parks and the Internet.

There are a number of important aspects that can be used to describe true commons. The first is that the commons cannot be commoditized – if they are, they cease to be commons.

The second aspect is that unlike private property, the commons is inclusive rather than exclusive — its nature is to share ownership as widely, rather than as narrowly, as possible.

The third aspect is that the assets in commons are meant to be preserved regardless of their return of capital. Just as we receive them as shared gifts, so we have a duty to pass them on to future generations in at least the same condition as we received them. If we can add to their value, so much the better, but at a minimum we must not degrade them, and we certainly have no right to destroy them.

The Public commons is commonly referred to as a place in our world that has a public good that is free for people to view and enjoy and owned by everyone who wants to be a part of it.

Something as simple as water and grass that you see in the park everyday is a public common. Most times people don't even realize that when they're in a park that it is free. However usually in these commons it is patrolled by other people in the area and if someone were to violate the commons in anyway by littering or dumping then it would be up to people in the area to control what happens to their own place.

Some people don't tend to agree with Peter Barnes in saying that the commons is all owned by the people because things like public transportation, public education and health care aren't always available to people.

For each of these mentioned things each of them has a "care penalty" in which there is a certain fee or tax to use these things provided by the government. This type of common is provided by a certain infrastructure like the government but to have access to it there is taxes on families and health insurance premiums.

Another highly used public common is the Internet. The Internet is something many people have access to as a resource and a scholarly tool but is also privatized as well. This type of common is a hybrid. To gain access to the Internet a household needs an Internet service provider that they have to pay in order to get online.

You now have seen the Definition of the Commons. Lets move to talk about the first five presidents. Why you may asked, simple reason they were all part of the founding fathers and had much to do we setting this country in direction that brings us to present day.

How many of us know who were the first five Presidents of this country? They were all part of the Founding Fathers.

Let's meet them and review some of my favorite quotes from each.

From Wikipedia, the free encyclopedia:

George Washington:

George Washington (February 22, 1732 [O.S. February 11, 1731] – December 14, 1799) was the first President of the United States of America, serving from 1789 to 1797, and the dominant military and political leader of the United States from 1775 to 1799.

He led the American victory over Great Britain in the American Revolutionary War as commander-in-chief of the Continental Army from 1775 to 1783, and presided over the writing of the Constitution in 1787.

Washington became the first president, by unanimous choice, and oversaw the creation of a strong, well-financed national government that maintained neutrality in the wars raging in Europe, suppressed rebellion, and won acceptance among Americans of all types.

His leadership style established many forms and rituals of government that have been used since, such as using a cabinet system and delivering an inaugural address. Washington is universally regarded as the "Father of his country."

Some of my Favorite quotes from George Washington:

"The basis of our political system is the right of the people to make and to alter their constitutions of government."
George Washington

"Experience teaches us that it is much easier to prevent an enemy from posting themselves than it is to dislodge them after they have got possession."
George Washington

With the current GOP bent on turning this county into a Fascist Nation, I see this coming election as the last chance to save this country from a takeover and the end of Democracy.

"It may be laid down as a primary position, and the basis of our system, that every Citizen who enjoys the protection of a Free Government, owes not only a proportion of his property, but even of his personal services to the defense of it."
George Washington

This is telling you that Washington wanted America to advance and that can only happen if the people of this country contribute to it to maintain the Commons. The Current GOP has been taken over by the Banks and Greed. What they want is to end the giving of anything to the Commons but reaping all the benefits of the Commons while taking control and ending the Commons.

"I have no other view than to promote the public good, and am unambitious of honors not founded in the approbation of my Country."
George Washington

This statement should be read to every single Politician that is sworn into Office. Now that we have Citizen United and Democracy is for sale we will see little or no Honor of the people that elected them and nothing but allegiance to Greed.

"Honor a simple word for a complex world. I once thought that our elected officials felt it would be a honor to serve those who elected them to office. With the current GOP we see no honor and we see no compassion for the people that elected them. What we see is tyranny, as they seek to destroy America in the hope people will blame President Obama and put the GOP back in Power."
Jeff Carlson

From Wikipedia, the free encyclopedia:

John Adams

John Adams (October 30, 1735 (O.S. October 19, 1735) – July 4, 1826) was an American Founding Father, and the second President of the United States (1797–1801).

He was also a lawyer, statesman, diplomat, political theorist, and a leading champion of independence in 1776.

Hailing from New England, Adams, a prominent lawyer and public figure in Boston, was highly educated and represented Enlightenment values promoting republicanism.

A Federalist, he was highly influential and one of the key Founding Fathers of the United States.

Adams came to prominence in the early stages of the American Revolution. As a delegate from Massachusetts to the Continental Congress, he played a leading role in persuading Congress to declare independence and assisted Thomas Jefferson in drafting the Declaration of Independence.

As a diplomat in Europe, he was a major negotiator of the eventual peace treaty with Great Britain, and chiefly responsible for obtaining important loans from Amsterdam bankers.

A political theorist and historian, Adams largely wrote the Massachusetts Constitution in 1780 which soon after ended slavery in Massachusetts, but was in Europe when the federal Constitution was drafted on similar principles later in the decade.

One of his greatest roles was as a judge of character: in 1775, he nominated George Washington to be commander-in-chief, and 25 years later nominated John Marshall to be Chief Justice of the United States.

Some of my Favorite quotes from John Adams.

"I must study politics and war that my sons may have liberty to study mathematics and philosophy."
John Adams

This quotes hits home so many ways.
You could see his hope for this country was that education and the growing of the Commons would lead to a better future for his Kids and Grand Kids. The current GOP wants this country in constant war and they want to end Public Education that would end the hope for millions.

"Our Constitution was made only for a moral and religious people. It is wholly inadequate to the government of any other."
John Adams

America is one of the most Religious countries in the world so that portion rings true. The breakdown of our Morals especially in Politics has put Democracy at risk.

"Power always thinks... that it is doing God's service when it is violating all his laws."
John Adams

Now if you listen to GOP they use this all the time, "GOD told me to do it". Adams was very religious and I can bet he rolls over in his grave every time the current GOP speaks.

"The Declaration of Independence I always considered as a theatrical show. Jefferson ran away with all the stage effect of that... and all the glory of it."
John Adams

You could see how Adams and Jefferson had a great rivalry and yes Jefferson was the showman of the Founding Fathers.

From Wikipedia, the free encyclopedia:

Thomas Jefferson

Thomas Jefferson (April 13, 1743 (April 2, 1743 O.S.) – July 4, 1826) was an American Founding Father, the principal author of the Declaration of Independence (1776) and the third President of the United States (1801–1809).

At the beginning of the American Revolution, He served in the Continental Congress, representing Virginia and then served as a wartime Governor of Virginia (1779–1781).

Just after the war ended, from mid-1784 Jefferson served as a diplomat, stationed in Paris, to help negotiate commercial treaties. In May 1785, he became the United States Minister to France. Jefferson was the first United States Secretary of State (1790–1793) serving under President George Washington.

Upon resigning his office, with his close friend James Madison he organized the Democratic-Republican Party. Elected Vice-President in 1796, when he came in second to John Adams of the Federalists, Jefferson with Madison secretly wrote the Kentucky and Virginia Resolutions, which attempted to nullify the Alien and Sedition Acts.

Elected president in what Jefferson called the Revolution of 1800, he oversaw a peaceful transition in power, purchased the vast Louisiana Territory from France

(1803), and sent the Lewis and Clark Expedition (1804–1806) to explore the new west.

His second term was beset with troubles at home, such as the failed treason trial of his former Vice President Aaron Burr, and escalating trouble with Britain. With Britain at war with Napoleon, he tried aggressive economic warfare against them; however, his embargo laws did more damage to American trade and the economy.

Jefferson has often been rated in scholarly surveys as one of the greatest U.S. presidents, though since the mid-twentieth century, some historians have increasingly criticized him for his failure to act against domestic slavery.

A leader in the Enlightenment, Jefferson was a polymath who spoke five languages and was deeply interested in science, invention, architecture, religion and philosophy, interests that led him to the founding of the University of Virginia after his presidency.

Some of my Favorite quotes from Thomas Jefferson: (Note Jefferson, by far was the most quoted of our presidents and had a sense on how to reach into the future with wisdom for all ages.)

"I believe that banking institutions are more dangerous to our liberties than standing armies. "
Thomas Jefferson

Jefferson, like all the founding fathers feared the Banks and Corporations more than any Army. He would be sick to death over how the GOP is under total control of the Corporations and because of Citizen United just might end all liberty, and America will be a Fascist nation controlled by the Rich using a authoritarian rule under the name of GOD.

"A Bill of Rights is what the people are entitled to against every government, and what no just government should refuse, or rest on inference."
Thomas Jefferson

Jefferson had such a great vision of where this country should go.

"All tyranny needs to gain a foothold is for people of good conscience to remain silent."
Thomas Jefferson

"I have sworn upon the altar of God, eternal hostility against every form of tyranny over the mind of man."
Thomas Jefferson

"A government afraid of its citizens is a Democracy. Citizens afraid of government is tyranny!"
Thomas Jefferson

We see how Jefferson feared the Tyranny of man as a sure way to the death of Democracy.

Here is a write up of mine after seeing the nasty things the GOP were doing to this country to undermine it and destroy all that has been fought for all these years.

What is Tyranny: By Jeff Carlson

I see a Party that sold its soul to Devil (Grover Norquist) --- WHY do they FEAR this Man? 238 House members and 41 Senators have taken the pledge. On the state level, 13 governors and 1249 state legislators have taken the pledge.

I look at the Party of Scrooge / Tea Baggers / Republicans
and what I see is a party that uses HATE, FEAR and LIES.

They used blackmail to get tax breaks for the upper 1%.

I see a party that used blackmail and held the American
people hostage and got our Credit status lowered.

I see a Party that sabotage, the Post Office.

I see a Party that has implemented Voter Suppression every state they could.

I see a Party that has gone after unions, teachers, and children.

I see a Party out to destroy the EPA and FDA

I see a Party Attacking women's rights in every state they control and at the national level.

I see a Party that if they win in 2012 will go straight to a WAR in IRAN using LIES because they OWN the MEDIA and they know they can.

I see a Party wanting to sell off our National Parks and all our infrastructure things like the water that we need to live on.

I see a party that cares so little about the American people that it will do nothing to create jobs and in fact is going all out to eliminate jobs.

All of this is because of a hatred they have for a president that for over 3 years tried to work with them. This has angered President Obama's own base. This Man, President Obama, is no longer a Sleeping Dog and has shown some Bite.

Tyranny is all that fits what this Party has been doing and this country needs to be educated and informed and we must end this Tyranny in November 2012.

From Wikipedia, the free encyclopedia:

James Madison

James Madison, Jr. (March 16, 1751 (O.S. March 5) – June 28, 1836) was an American statesman and political theorist, the fourth President of the United States (1809–1817). He is hailed as the "Father of the Constitution" for being instrumental in the drafting of the United States Constitution and as the key champion and author of the United States Bill of Rights.

He served as a politician much of his adult life. Like other Virginia statesmen in the slave society, he was a slaveholder and part of the élite; he inherited his plantation known as Montpelier, and owned hundreds of slaves during his lifetime to cultivate tobacco and other crops.

After the constitution had been drafted, Madison became one of the leaders in the movement to ratify it. His collaboration with Alexander Hamilton and John Jay produced the Federalist Papers (1788). Circulated only in New York at the time, they would later be considered among the most important polemics in support of the Constitution.

He was also a delegate to the Virginia constitutional ratifying convention, and was instrumental to the successful ratification effort in Virginia. Like most of his contemporaries, Madison changed his political views during his life. During the drafting and ratification of the constitution, he favored a strong national government, though later he grew to favor stronger state governments, before settling between the two extremes late in his life.

In 1789, Madison became a leader in the new House of Representatives, drafting many basic laws. He is notable for drafting the first ten amendments to the Constitution, and thus is known as the "Father of the Bill of Rights".

Madison worked closely with President George Washington to organize the new federal government. Breaking with Hamilton and what became the Federalist party in 1791, Madison and Thomas Jefferson organized what they called the Republican Party (later called by historians the Democratic-Republican Party) in opposition to key policies of the Federalists, especially the national bank and the Jay Treaty. He co-authored, along with Thomas Jefferson, the Kentucky and Virginia Resolutions in 1798 to protest the Alien and Sedition Acts.

Some of my Favorite quotes from James Madison:

"The purpose of separation of church and state is to keep forever from these shores the ceaseless strife that has soaked the soil of Europe with blood for centuries."
James Madison

Many people came to America for this very reason to flee Religious Persecution and the endless wars caused by Religion

"And I have no doubt that every new example will succeed, as every past one has done, in showing that religion and Government will both exist in greater purity, the less they are mixed together."
James Madison

Here again Madison states keep religion out of politics.

"If Tyranny and Oppression come to this land, it will be in the guise of fighting a foreign enemy".
James Madison

Madison, looking at the future and he just be talking about if the GOP win in November they will use the War they start in IRAN to lock down this country and take Liberty away from the people.

"Each generation should be made to bear the burden of its own wars, instead of carrying them on, at the expense of other generations."
James Madison

The Bush Administration never read this quote. They fought two wars unfunded and we to this day are paying for his wars and his mess.

From Wikipedia, the free encyclopedia:

James Monroe

James Monroe (April 28, 1758 – July 4, 1831) was the fifth President of the United States (1817–1825). Monroe was the last president who was a Founding Father of the United States, and the last president from the Virginia dynasty and the Republican Generation.

His presidency was marked both by an "Era of Good Feelings" – a period of relatively little partisan strife – and later by the Panic of 1819 and a fierce national debate over the admission of the Missouri Territory.

Monroe is most noted for his proclamation of the Monroe Doctrine in 1823, which stated that the United States would not tolerate further European intervention in the Americas.

Born in Westmoreland County, Virginia, Monroe fought in the American Revolutionary War. He was injured in the Battle of Trenton with a musket ball to his shoulder.

After studying law under Thomas Jefferson from 1780 to 1783, he served as a delegate in the Continental Congress. As an anti-federalist delegate to the Virginia convention that considered ratification of the United States Constitution, Monroe opposed ratification, claiming it gave too much power to the central government. Nonetheless, Monroe took an active part in the new government and in 1790 he was elected to the Senate of the first United States Congress, where he joined the Jeffersonians.

He gained experience as an executive as the Governor of Virginia and rose to national prominence when as a diplomat in France he helped negotiate the Louisiana Purchase in 1803. Monroe was of French and Scottish descent.

During the War of 1812, Monroe held the critical roles of Secretary of State and the Secretary of War under President James Madison.[2] Facing little opposition from the fractured Federalist Party, Monroe was easily elected president in 1816, winning over 80 percent of the electoral vote and becoming the last president during the First Party System era of American politics.

As president, he sought to ease partisan tensions and embarked on a tour of the country and was well received everywhere.[citation needed] As nationalism surged, partisan fury subsided and the "Era of Good Feelings" ensued until the Panic of 1819 struck and dispute over the admission of Missouri embroiled the country in 1820. Nonetheless, Monroe won near-unanimous reelection. In 1823, he announced the Monroe Doctrine, which became a landmark in American foreign policy. His presidency concluded the first period of American presidential history before the beginning of Jacksonian democracy and the Second Party System era. Following his retirement in 1825, Monroe was plagued by financial difficulties. He died in New York City on July 4, 1831.

Some of my Favorite quotes from James Monroe:

"If we look to the history of other nations, ancient or modern, we find no example of a growth so rapid, so gigantic, of a people so prosperous and happy."
James Monroe

What we see from this quote was America was on the move and public education was the key for this growth.   Now we have the GOP going all out to destroy public education.

"The public lands are a public stock, which ought to be disposed of to the best advantage for the nation."
James Monroe

What again Monroe was saying here for the good of the Nation and he surely was not talking about the good of the Corporation. Note the GOP does nothing but for the good of the Corporation.

"To impose taxes when the public exigencies require them is an obligation of the most sacred character, especially with a free people.'
James Monroe

All we hear from the Right is we have a spending problem but in reality what is going on is we have a revenue problem because of the spending on things not needed to support the Commons and its people.   Bush and his Nation Building is a prime example of mis-management of tax revenues.

"It is only when the people become ignorant and corrupt, when they degenerate into a populace, that they are incapable of exercising their sovereignty."
James Monroe

Again here is Monroe warning us of misinformation and lack of education. The GOP is in a all out effort to dumb down this country and we must not allow this to happen.

Education the mainstay of the Commons

Education will be my main focus when talking about the Commons, because right now in this country the GOP at all levels is attacking public education.

Why we ask? There are two reasons:

The First reason is to destroy the unions. Unions are the only organized group that has any power to fight the Power of the Corporations. Citizen United has distorted the election process so much in this country that we may never see a fair election again. Making the 2012 election as the most important one in the history of this country.

The second reason is to end the Public Education system and go to a privatized voucher system.

You will hear much about how we should destroy he Public Education System and go to a Voucher System.

This would be a disaster that this country might not recover from and here is why:

1. By doing this the public will now be paying for the wealthy kids to go to Private Schools.

2. By allowing this you would see the Private Schools Cherry Pick the Students they want to attend their schools.

3. Control the Curriculum. We have seen in TEXAS and other states where the History Books are full of LIES. Joe McCarthy saved us from the COMMIES. We Won the Vietnam War. There were mass amounts of WMD found in IRAQ and BUSH saved America by attacking them.

4. Teachers and unions would take a huge hit. Religion and Right Wing Ideology would be rammed down the throats of our kids using every brainwashing method known to man to stop free thinking.

Here is a Quote from a Article talking about what Walker is doing to Wisconsin and it is not good.

Mike Langyel, the head of the Milwaukee Teachers' Education Association, as emotional in a phone call to discuss the budget proposal, which he called "a direct attack on public education in Milwaukee."

"In a time of budget cuts, the governor is going to subsidize the tuition of wealthy families by removing the income caps, so that will be an added burden to state government,"

What you see Walker doing in Wisconsin, is what the GOP would love to do all over the Country. Somehow I hope the people of this country are smart enough to figure out we do not want our schools privatized and only a few selected kids would be allowed to attend.

Here are some wonderful quotes about the School Voucher System:

"The real equity issue is that there are radically unequal allocations of funds to schools. These unequal allocations routinely disadvantage schools in central cities and in poor rural areas. Private school choice, as it is currently being proposed, is a smokescreen to avoid tackling this real equity issue."
--Linda Darling-Hammond, professor of teaching and teacher education at Stanford University.

"Voucher proposals take many forms, and some are designed to deliberately disguise the basic realities that will result over time. The best students will be skimmed off -- those whom private schools find desirable for their own reasons. Since families will have to make up additional costs, those in the upper-and middle-income brackets will be helped the most -- as long as their kids don't have personal, behavioral, or educational challenges that cause the private school to pass them by."
-- Kweisi Mfume, president and CEO of the NAACP

Our founding fathers wanted educated people and to have available the tools for learning in Public Libraries.

We must never abandon the public education system and destroy our public libraries.

"Educate and inform the whole mass of the people... They are the only sure reliance for the preservation of our liberty."
Thomas Jefferson

Jefferson like all the founding fathers wanted to make sure Americans were educated.

"A library, to modify the famous metaphor of Socrates, should be the delivery room for the birth of ideas – a place where history comes to life."
Norman Cousins (June 24, 1915 – November 30, 1990)
An American political journalist, author, professor, and world peace advocate.

What you see whenever the GOP take control is the censorship or the closing of Libraries.

"Books constitute capital. A library book lasts as long as a house, for hundreds of years. It is not, then, an article of mere consumption but fairly of capital, and often in the case of professional men, setting out in life, it is their only capital."
Thomas Jefferson

Again Jefferson, knowing that the educated person is the capital of a great nation.

"Knowledge will forever govern ignorance; and a people who mean to be their own governors must arm themselves with the power which knowledge gives."
James Madison

"Learned Institutions ought to be favorite objects with every free people. They throw that light over the public mind which is the best security against crafty and dangerous encroachments on the public liberty."
James Madison

"Every nation whose affairs betray a want of wisdom and stability may calculate on every loss which can be sustained from the more systematic policy of its wiser neighbors."
James Madison

Madison, like Jefferson felt that education was the key for people to understand what is expected of their elected officials and sadly I think in today's terms the American people lack the knowledge and are easily lead by the Media.

"If anybody wanted to photograph my life, they'd get bored in a day. 'Here's Matt at home learning his lines. Here's Matt researching in aisle six of his local library'. A few hours of that and they'd go home."
Matt Damon

Matt Damon, a strong supporter of education and the libraries of this country and dead set against a voucher school system.

"The power of words whether it is the Spoken or Written word transcends the human race. Walk through the doors of a library and you have opened the doors to History, Love, Adventure, Science and all our Cultures. Read the words of books and it will open your eyes forever."
Jeff Carlson

As you watch the GOP, you see that it is a party that wants to control education control what you read control what you watch. They would want to monitor the libraries allowing only what they want you to read. Or just out right close the Libraries. They like all fascist consider education and the ability to select your own reading materials as a enemy to all their ideologies.

This is what the Nazi's did when they took over Germany. They used Religion and Fear to take over the Education System and strip the Libraries and control the Message (words) so that people had little to go on to make valid decisions.

Water control under attack

What could more the Commons than Water. I have been reading many articles about water and how the Giant Corporations are working hard to take total control of the Water Systems in this country and around the World.

I have been reading about Water and Fracking and what I see is America heading to a disaster for all and the Republican Party is behind the destruction caused by Fracking.

At this time we have many Republican governors are working hard to privatize the Water Utilities in the states they control.

Lets connect DOTS again Fracking takes millions of gallons of water to do its job that water is then left worthless and full of chemicals. Soon there will be little clean water left for not only humans but for all living things.

Do you want Koch Industries the Masters of our Water?

This is what the Republicans will be pushing all over the country.

Fracking bill written by **ALEC** and backed by the **Republican Party!!**

Ohio SB 315: "This clause, as written, gags doctors from notifying the health department of possible contamination and exposure to the public to these chemicals. This does not protect Ohio citizens public health but it protects the oil and gas industry from liability."

Notice that the Republican bill eliminates all Liability from the corporations that will poison the water and make us our kids and grand kids ill and then the Corporations will walk leaving us to Die.

"Water, creatures both large and small seek out this gift from god. Water, is the source to all life. Water, should be shared by all, Water should never come under the control of mankind seeking profits"
Jeff Carlson

"In this country and around the world there are many that seek out the control of our precious water. We must never allow the Commons to become privatized or we will live under the power of tyrants."
Jeff Carlson

Article written by USA Today:
"Wyoming's smog exceeds Los Angeles' due to fracking -
Residents who live near the gas fields in the state's western corner are complaining of watery eyes, shortness of breath and bloody noses.
The cause is clearer than the air: local ozone levels recently exceeded the highest levels recorded in the biggest U.S. cities last year."

I wrote this quote to go with a picture of a Purple Butterfly touching water:

"The Beauty of the Butterfly and the touch of cool clean water are truly Gods gift to Humans. As right wing ideology (profits before people) and fracking consume more and more our water resources it might mean the death to the butterfly and just maybe the death to all humans."
Jeff Carlson

There is a proverb 6:6-8 "Go unto the ant... See her ways and be wise; it has not commander or ruler, yet it stores its provisions in summer and gathers its food at harvest"

I dedicate this quote to the Ant:

"Give me the strength and tenacity of the Ant to overcome the obstacles that we face in order to move this world to a better place than what we inherited"
Jeff Carlson

Shakespeare telling us something that most of us never take the time to listen to, our wonderful planet Earth.

"The earth has music for those who listen."
Shakespeare

"Right now man, is not treating this planet with the respect and diligence needed for this planet to survive, we do not hear the crying or feel the tears of this great planet earth."
Jeff Carlson

Got to ask, do we want to control our environment and infrastructure or turn it over the private corporations to exploit us.

What kind of world do we want for our Kids, our Grand Kids, all creatures want to protect their own, we must do every thing in our power to save our water, to save our environment, from the most destructive source on earth, Man"
Jeff Carlson

I wrote that quote after spending the day with my Grand Kids. I came home determined to do everything I can to inform the country that corporations are killing the environment and eventually will kill us all, and what for to make more money than any person could ever spend and surly will be buried with the American Dream gone wrong.

"At one time there was this proud and mighty country called America, we built bridges across vast amounts of rivers, mountains and even oceans. This America took care of its Infrastructure, but now after thirty years of right wing ideology our Infrastructure is crumbling, in many of the right wing states, being sold off to the highest bidder."
Jeff Carlson

We have seen over and over where the Republicans block any attempt at getting the infrastructure worked on therefore creating millions of jobs. They have only one thing on their agenda and that is to destroy the economy and make President Obama, take the blame for their misgivings.

It is time all Americans see the reality of, we are one nation and "We are the people" must prevail over "We the Corporation" or we will be heading to nothing but disaster.

This is what I call our Commons and they are under attack by giant corporations and those corporations control the Republican Party. Their agenda is to take control of the peoples Commons. This is against everything our founding fathers stood for. Profits before People that is the Republican Agenda.

Know your enemy
They are right here in America Hiding in plain sight

Lets start with the Republican Party normally I would not call them a enemy but the damage they are doing to America, I have to call them what they are.

"For the first time in my life I can say that the 2012 GOP / Tea Party / Party of Scrooge has become the number one enemy and danger to the American Way."
Jeff Carlson

Lets take a look back before we look at the current Republicans.

Here was a write up I called "Who did this" and understand all these things were a positive for the Republican Party as their goal is to end he NEW DEAL and set up a third world country under a Fascist Government.

WHO DID THIS: Accountability - 2000 to 2006

Who ignored intelligence reports that repeated over and over that Al-Qaeda is going to launch a terrorist attack on America Using Hijacked Air Planes?

Who Lied and led us into two wars and never funded them?

Who then gave tax breaks to the richest people in the country while the Wars raged on?

Who passed Medicare Part D at a cost of a trillion dollars a year to the American taxpayers and did not fund it?

Who allowed 47,000 manufacturing plants to close and 3 million people to lose their jobs, while paying these Corporations over 1 trillion to do this?

Who allowed Wall Street to destroy the American economy while keeping a closed eye to all the signals that something was wrong?

Who put a Poison Pill into the Post Office in a effort to destroy a American Icon that has served America from the days that our country was founded?

Who turned over an economy in ruins with 700,000 Americans losing their Jobs each Month and said "Mission Accomplished."

Bush accomplished what he set out to do destroy the Middle Class in this country.

Here is a quote from IKE we all need to read and pass on to all our friends especially your republican friends:

"Should any political party attempt to abolish social security, unemployment insurance, and eliminate labor laws and farm programs, you would not hear of that party again in our political history. There is a tiny splinter group, of course, that believes that you can do these things. Among them are a few Texas oil millionaires, and an occasional politician or businessman from other areas. Their number is negligible and they are stupid."
Dwight D. Eisenhower (1890–1969)

Can you imagine what Eisenhower would be thinking if he saw the 2012 version of his Party.

Lets talk about Fear because of all the things the GOP do this is their Mainstay to control of their base.

Some of my favorite Quotes about " FEAR "

"It's fear of the unknown. The unknown is what it is. And to be frightened of it is what sends everybody scurrying around chasing dreams, illusions, wars, peace, love, hate, all that--it's all illusion. Unknown is what it is. Accept that it's unknown and it's plain sailing. Everything is unknown--then you're ahead of the game. That's what it is. Right?"
 John Lennon quotes (English Singer, Songwriter and Political activist, member of the "Beatles", 1940-1980)

"Conservatism is a partially heritable personality trait that predisposes some people to be cognitively inflexible, fond of hierarchy, and inordinately afraid of uncertainty, change, and death. People vote Republican because Republicans offer "moral clarity"—a simple vision of good and evil that activates deep seated fears in much of the electorate."
 Jonathan Haidt, Associate Professor of Psychology at the University of Virginia.

"They who can give up essential liberty to obtain a little temporary safety, deserve neither liberty nor safety."
Quote from Benjamin Franklin (1818):
Note: This was written by Franklin, within quotation marks but is generally accepted as his original thought, sometime shortly before February 17, 1775 as part of his notes for a proposition at the Pennsylvania Assembly, as published in Memoirs of the life and writings of Benjamin Franklin (1818).

Fear is one of the Main Stays of the GOP:
**Fear Obama because he is a Muslim,
**Fear Obama because he is a Socialist,
**Fear Obama because he is going to take your guns away
**Fear Obama because he is going to run the Deficits up.

They feed these Lies to the Base through Fox News and Rush Limbaugh and his right wing talking head friends.

"What the GOP fear most is that we get educated and informed.
So we know the lies when we see them. Knowledge is the foil to Fear."
Jeff Carlson

The GOP loves to use FEAR to take your rights away in the Name of we will protect you. The Patriot Act came out of fear.

The **USA PATRIOT Act** (commonly known as the Patriot Act) is an Act of the U.S. Congress that was signed into law by President George W. Bush on October 26, 2001. The title of the act is a ten letter backronym (USA PATRIOT) that stands for Uniting (and) Strengthening America (by) Providing Appropriate Tools Required (to) Intercept (and) Obstruct Terrorism Act of 2001.

The Act was passed in the House by 357 to 66 (of 435) and in the Senate by 98 to 1, with Russ Feingold the only opposition.

Opponents of the law have criticized its authorization of indefinite detentions of immigrants; searches through which law enforcement officers search a home or business without the owner's or the occupant's permission or knowledge; the expanded use of National Security Letters, which allows the Federal Bureau of Investigation (FBI) to search telephone, e-mail, and financial records without a court order, and the expanded access of law enforcement agencies to business records, including library and financial records. Since its passage, several legal challenges have been brought against the act, and Federal courts have ruled that a number of provisions are unconstitutional.

A young man, Trayvon Martin, was gunned down in Florida because of Fear. The man who killed him did it out of Hate and Fear.

Hate and Fear are always being pushed on Fox News and by Rush Limbaugh and his right wing talking head friends.

"Fear just the word scares some people, Fear is the unknown, Some people use Fear to control others, Some people live their whole lives in Fear. Knowledge is the foil to Fear. We must all seek out that Knowledge that unlocks our Fears."
Jeff Carlson

Here is one of my Quotes of the Day **"The American Dream"**
BY: Bob Taft an Ohio Republican Party politician.

Robert Alphonso Taft was born on September 8, 1889, in Cincinnati, into one of Ohio's most famous political families. His grandfather, Alphonso, had been President Ulysses S. Grant's secretary of war. His father was William Howard Taft, later to become the 19th president of the United States.

"Everything depends on a good job - strong families, strong communities, the pursuit of the American dream, and a tax base to support schools for our kids and services for our seniors."
Bob Taft

 It was right around my birthday I sat back and I had thoughts on the American Dream and I came across this Quote from Bob Taft. Taft a true conservative and comes from nothing but a long line of ultra conservatives.

This quote is the American Dream and then I realized everything in this Quote is being attacked, opposed and destroyed by the current Republicans / Tea Party / Party of Scrooge.

Shows you that even their own party members have no clue the damage they are causing to the current recovery and the opportunity for all Americans to have a shot at the American Dream.

Here is a Poem I wrote about the American Dream:

I ONCE WAS PART OF THE AMERICAN DREAM

I am no one, I am everyone, and I am an American.
I once was part of the American Dream.

I had a good job with a corporation that had pride in its employees;
I was proud to be working for that corporation.

I owned a home where my kids could get a good education.
I watched them grow and wanted the American Dream for them.

Something changed... and it was called 'Right Wing Ideology'.
At first it was subtle, but soon it was obvious; things were not right.

They called it 'Mergers and Acquisitions', but in reality, your once proud corporation was getting bought out by a even larger corporation.

Employees now work longer hours, no longer with pride, but with fear.
The new corporation is always looking to outsource your job.

Soon your job becomes a number, and that number will be getting sent overseas.
Your job is gone, your pride is gone, and soon, your home and your health are gone.

Thirty years of Right Wing Ideology has dismantled the middle class.
Right Wing Ideology has ended the American Dream for me my Kids and my Grand Kids.

I am no one, I am everyone, and I am an American.
I once was part of the American Dream.

By Jeff Carlson

If you start to look at the Policies of the Republicans you can see there is not much in it for the working people, seniors and sadly veterans returning from the Wars started by the Republican Party.

"Greed, Hate, and No Compassion for their fellow humans is the mark of the Modern Social Conservative."
Jeff Carlson

Lets talk about the Ryan Bill and Austerity because the Republicans are basing their entire economy on Austerity. This is the kind of Austerity that is currently killing just about every single European Country.

Austerity:
From Wikipedia, the free encyclopedia:

In economics, austerity is a policy of deficit-cutting, lower spending, and a reduction in the amount of benefits and public services provided. Austerity, policies are often used by governments to reduce their deficit spending. While sometimes coupled with increases in taxes to pay back creditors to reduce debt.

Here are some quotes about Austerity going on in Europe;

The Right promised that if you do Austerity all would be good, Debt would go down and jobs created It was a total LIE and has been a disaster where ever it was done.

"Far from falling, debt burdens are rising fastest in European countries that have enacted the most draconian austerity programs, according to The Associated Press' Global Economy Tracker, which monitors the performance of 30 major economies. The numbers back up what many analysts say: Austerity isn't just painful. It can be counterproductive and even make a country's debt load grow."
Bill Bonner, for the Daily Reckoning

In Europe, official opinion is slowly beginning to recognize the medicine prescribed isn't working. The International Monetary Fund — and ironically officials at the credit rating agency Standard and Poor's — have warned of the dangers of premature severe cuts.

"In comparison, the United States has fared better, with its economy enjoying slow growth and jobs beginning to reappear. But even here the austerian fallacies had ruinous effect. The president's initial recovery plan was too small. It stopped the free fall of the economy but did not make up for the collapse of consumer demand and the drastic cuts in state and local government spending and employment. Wall Street was saved, but virtually nothing has been done for homeowners, the biggest victims of Wall Street's excesses."
Katrina Vanden Heuve

The Filibuster:

"The Filibuster has been used by the Republicans, as a weapon to make sure America is not moving and recovering from the Disaster the Republicans caused under Bush. Since the Day President Obama took office, the Republicans have vowed that they would destroy America in order to make President Obama a one term president"
Jeff Carlson

Is the filibuster unconstitutional?
Posted by Ezra Klein 05/15/2012

According to Best Lawyers — "the oldest and most respected peer-review publication in the legal profession" — Emmet Bondurant "is the go-to lawyer when a business person just can't afford to lose a lawsuit." He was its 2010 Lawyer of the Year for Antitrust and Bet-the-Company Litigation. But now, he's bitten off something even bigger: bet-the-country litigation.

Bondurant thinks the filibuster is unconstitutional. And, alongside Common Cause, where he serves on the board of directors, he's suing to have the Supreme Court abolish it.

(Graph: Todd Lindeman; Data: Senate.gov) In a 2011 article in the Harvard Law School's Journal on Legislation, Bondurant laid out his case for why the filibuster crosses constitutional red lines. But to understand the argument, you have to understand the history: The filibuster was a mistake.

Mitch McConnell: **"The single most important thing we want to achieve is for President Obama to be a one-term president."**

MSNBC host Joe Scarborough (a republican) was floored by McConnell's open admission that his single most important goal is to defeat Obama. "Mitch McConnell said that?!? ... He admitted that on the record?!? That is embarrassing," he said. "Can I just say for the record – that is pathetic."

A rule permitting cloture — a move to end debate and move to a vote — was adopted in 1917 with two-thirds of those voting needed to move the question. The current 60-vote requirement to invoke cloture was introduced in 1975. In the early 1970s the Senate established a two-track system, which permitted lawmakers to consider other legislation while a bill was being filibustered — effectively ending the practice requiring those blocking consideration to remain on the floor in sometimes marathon sessions.

The most famous filibusters came in the late 1950s and early 1960s over civil rights legislation. Sen. Strom Thurmond of South Carolina holds the record for a filibuster, maintaining the floor for 24 hours and 18 minutes during consideration of the Civil Rights Act of 1957, which eventually passed.

Regardless, for most of its history the filibuster was a seldom used tool. From 1917 to 1970 cloture was invoked 58 times. During the 92nd Congress in 1971-72 the number suddenly jumped to 24. But the real increase began with the 110th Congress in 2007-2008 when 139 cloture motions were filed — the all-time high. The 111th Congress in 2009-2010 was almost as busy with 137 cloture motions filed. Thus far in the 112th Congress there have been 86 cloture motions.

"The GOP is a Party that does not care about seniors, Workers, Women, Kids, Science, Education or the Environment. What they stand for if Control, Power and Greed."
Jeff Carlson

A special note goes to Mitch McConnell, John Boehner and Eric Cantor.

The Day after President Obama was elected these Republican leaders got together with some other leaders of their Party and vowed that they would do everything they could to stop the economy from growing so that they can blame the President and again gain control of the Country in which their policies caused the depression we have been struggling to get out of.

This is a quote I wrote after I had discovered the treason these republicans have committed:

"Honor a simple word for a complex world. I once thought that our elected officials felt it would be a honor to serve those who elected them to office. With the current Republicans we see no honor and we see no compassion for the people that elected them. What we see is tyranny, as they seek to destroy America in the hope people will blame Obama and put the Republicans back in Power."
Jeff Carlson

What amazes me is that the Mainstream Media no longer seems to challenge the lies and distortions that come from the Republican Party and because of that we got the Tea Party now controlling the House and making one big mess of the whole country.

Here is a quote I wrote that I think really hits home with most Americans. I know many of my friends that are Republican would never vote for them if they actually understood the agenda of the Republican Party but that agenda is never allowed to be talk about in the Mainstream Media:

"We are a society that is so overwhelmed with surviving the day to day struggles we do not keep track of the things our government is doing. The Republicans exploits this using Fox News and the Talking Radio shows to misinform and plain out right Lie to keep Americans from making informed decisions when it comes to voting on the issues that can harm them."
Jeff Carlson

Here are a few of my favorite quotes to go with misinformation:

"The lowest form of popular culture - lack of information, misinformation, disinformation, and a contempt for the truth or the reality of most people's lives - has overrun real journalism. Today, ordinary Americans are being stuffed with garbage."
Carl Bernstein, American Writer

"A society that's misinformed is a dangerous society. The leader that makes decisions based on misinformation is very dangerous."
Laksamana Sukardi, Writer and Politician from Indonesia

"Like it or not, we're still a primitive tribe ruled by fears, superstition and misinformation."
Bill Maher (American Comedian, Actor, Writer and Producer. b.1956)

Now lets take a look back to 2010 when the Republicans using the LIE of "JOBS JOBS JOBS" got swept into office in places that would never allow Republicans.

Republicans took advantage of this and have rammed in ALEC Written Bills such as "Right to Work", "Voter ID", "Tort Reform" and many other social agendas that most people do not agree with.

Since they were elected in 2010 they have been responsible for eliminating nearly 2.5 million jobs. Those jobs almost all union jobs are your teachers, state workers, fire and police. All this was being done for two reasons. One to undercut the economy and the second is to crush the unions.

I have seen the Republicans are back at it again talking about the economy and "JOBS JOBS JOBS" are we going to fall for the same lies all over? See my quote about misinformation sadly most people are just to busy to realize just how bad the Republicans deceive the American People.

In my issues chapter, I will go over all the issues and where the Democrats stand and where the Republicans stand.

"The difference between the Democrats and the Republicans is that people on the left want to know and people on the right are afraid to ask"
Jeff Carlson

If you are a Republican you just are not allowed to think you are expected to fall in line without questions asked.

**"We as Republicans do not believe in science and nature.
We as Republicans will tell you what is real and what is not.
We as Republicans always know what's best for you.
We as Republicans will protect you from your fears ..."**
Jeff Carlson

"People that vote Republican never seek out the truth, what they seek out is any excuse to justify voting for people that will harm them"
Jeff Carlson.

Now we know that the Ticket for the Republicans is going to be Mitt Romney and Paul Ryan.

I really do not have anything good to say about either. Both men have been schooled in classes held by the Koch Industries and ALEC. What they learn in these classes is how to lie about the bills being pushed around the country by Republicans but really written by Alec and strong armed into place by the US Chamber of Commerce.

Mitt Romney:

This man is a plastic man that lies with ease for his Party that is based totally on lies, fear and misinformation.

I love this quote from Plato that rings true in the world of Politics today.

"Those who are too smart to engage in politics are punished by being governed by those who are dumber."
Plato (Ancient Greek Philosopher He was the world's most influential philosopher. 428 BC-348 BC)

Plato, I am almost certain was talking about the Republican Party and specifically Romney. After watching his disaster in Europe while Olympics were going on was a classic screw up all over Europe making the leaders of our allies praying daily that Obama wins. To be honest I would say all the free world will be praying hard that Romney is not elected and America does not have another George Bush type of Leader.

Here is a Article written by: Jo Ann Brown about how she thinks Romney, will destroy America that I think needs to be put out there so we can see just what kind of man he is:

Don't Let Romney Break America

Naming a child is a delicate process. We purchase books on the subject that defines the meanings of a name. We sometimes choose a beloved family member's name. But how many people name their children after a friend. How close of a friendship does one has to be chosen as the name to be assigned to their child? George Romney, GOP candidate Willard Mitt Romney's father, named him after hotel magnate John Willard Marriott and his cousin Milton "Mitt" Romney, a former quarterback for the Chicago Bears.

George Romney and John Marriott's friendship and connections with Rollins, Gardeners and other members of the Mormon Church have formed a financial bulwark and support network for Mr. Romney at every important point in his political career. Starting with his 1994 Senate race, moving into the 2002 Salt Lake City Olympics effort that became his political springboard and continuing through his first foray into presidential politics, they have been there to open doors, provide seed money and rally support. To take one concrete measure of their support, records show that roughly two dozen members of Mormon families provided nearly $8 million of the financing for the "Super Pac" working to elect Mr. Romney, Restore Our Future, putting them in league with its Wall Street, real estate and energy donors. Prominent Mormons including David G. Neeleman, the JetBlue founder, and Eric Varvel, the chief executive officer of the banking division at Credit Suisse, are on his finance team. Many of Mr. Romney's major Mormon backers are tied to businesses with robust agendas in Washington — lobbying on tax, aviation and tourism policy, according to federal filings — and have something to gain by having a friend in the White House. In 1971, he earned a Bachelor of Arts from Brigham Young University and, in 1975, a joint Juris Doctor and Master of Business Administration from Harvard University. Romney entered the management consulting industry, and in 1977 secured a position at Bain & Company. In 1984, he co-founded and led the spin-off Bain Capital. To free up money to invest in the new business, founder Bill

Bain and his partners cashed out much of their stock in the consulting firm leaving it saddled with about $200 million in debt.

Bain &Company got into deep financial trouble partly because the founding partners of Bain Capital had stripped it of cash and saddled it with debt. "Mitt Romney's business man reputation was on the line. Bain sold top-dollar strategic advice to big businesses about how to protect them from going bust. If Bain & Company went bankrupt, "anyone associated with them would have looked clownish." Even though Bain & Company was deep in debt the firm was actually flush with cash. But Bain had inserted a poison pill in its loan agreement with the banks: Instead of being required to use its cash to pay back the firm's creditors, the money could be pocketed by Bain executives in the form of fat bonuses – starting with VPs making $200,000 and up. The bonus loophole gave Romney a perverse form of leverage.

Romney managed to convince Bain's creditors to take a steep discount on Bain debt, using a threat to pay Bain executives big bonuses that would have stripped it of the cash it had left, leaving creditors with next to nothing. One of those creditors was the FDIC, which had taken over a bank that loaned money to Bain. The FDIC ended up collecting about $14 million of the $30 million Bain owed it. Taxpayers didn't foot the bill for this. Those costs were in turn probably absorbed by bank customers in the form of higher fees. Even as consumers took a loss, however, a small group of investors wound up getting a good deal in the bailout. Bain Capital – the very firm that had triggered the crisis in the first place – walked away with $4 million. That was the fee it charged Bain & Company for loaning the consulting firm the services of its chief executive – one Willard Mitt Romney.

While entrenched with the Bain & Company debacle, he served on the board of directors of Marriott International from 1993 to 2002 and again 2009 to 2011. During his tenure, six years, he chaired the board's audit committee. While Romney was on the board, Marriott engaged in a number of corporate tax avoidance schemes.

1. Son of Boss tax shelter: Marriott executed a Son of Boss trade in mid-1994 – a scheme that manufactures "a gigantic tax loss out of thin air" to offset actual gains "without any economic risk, cost, or loss." Marriott later filed a return claiming an artificial loss to lower the company's taxable income. Marriott implemented the Son of Boss tax shelter scheme, which resulted in the company claiming $71 million in losses that federal courts later ruled never existed. Son of Boss schemes were notorious, involving about 1,800 people and costing the IRS an estimated $6 billion, and was described as "perhaps the largest tax avoidance scheme in history."

2. "Spray and pray": Marriott purchased four synthetic fuel plants in 2001 in order to benefit from federal tax credits for synthetic fuels, a strategy which was dubbed "spray and pray". In 2002, the company legally claimed $159 million of those credits, reducing their effective tax rate to just 6.8 percent—far below the normal corporate rate of 35%. Even Sen. John McCain criticized Marriott's behavior: "One of the greatest beneficiaries of this tax shelter—and that is all that it is, a tax shelter—is a very profitable hotel chain: Marriott."

3. Profit-shifting to Luxembourg: In 2009, Marriott collected $229 million in revenue—primarily from royalty, licensing and franchising fees—at its Luxembourg subsidiary, Global Hospitality Licensing S.à.r.l. The subsidiary reported having only one employee. By the end of 2011, the company $451 million in offshore earnings that it left overseas to delay paying US income taxes. Under Romney's proposed corporate tax plan, Marriott would never have to pay U.S. taxes on those earnings.

4. Questionable deductions: The IRS challenged $1 billion in deductions Marriott took related to an employee from 2000 to 2002. The company eventually agreed to pay about $220 million of what it owed in income taxes, excise taxes, and interest to the IRS and a number of states.

Source:
http://www.npr.org/2012/04/05/150058865/for-romney-family-ties-to-marriott-heirs-pay-off
http://www.biography.com/people/j-willard-marriott-9399868
http://www.nytimes.com/2012/07/17/us/politics/support-for-romney-by-old-mormon-families.html?_r=1&pagewanted=all
http://www.barackobama.com/truth-team/entry/four-ways-romney-helped-marriott-avoid-paying-taxes/
http://www.rollingstone.com/politics/news/the-federal-bailout-that-saved-mitt-romney-20120829

Paul Ryan:

Catholics United, while the group's executive director, James Salt, said: "**This is not the time for political ideology to trump human dignity. The recently-released budget saddens me as it's clear Congressman Ryan continues to follow the teachings of Ayn Rand, not Jesus Christ.**"

FROM MOVE ON: RYAN'S VISION FOR AMERICA

Dear Move On member,

Paul Ryan is bad for America. He's anti-choice, and would give big tax cuts for millionaires, while raising taxes on the middle-class. He's a Tea Party favorite who takes donations from the billionaire Koch brothers, and he introduced one of harshest and most inhumane budgets in recent history. His ideological hero for many years called selfishness a virtue and charity an abomination.

But most people don't know just how bad Paul Ryan is. So we made this list of 10 things to know about Mitt Romney's Vice Presidential pick, Paul Ryan. Read it, then click here to share this list as an image on social media, or just forward this email! The future of America is on the line — from a woman's right to choose to our economy.

10 Things to know about Paul Ryan

1. His economic plan would cost America 1 million jobs in the first year. Ryan's proposed budget would cripple the economy. He'd slash spending deeply, which would not only slow job growth, but shock the economy and cost 1 million of us our jobs in 2013 alone and kill more than 4 million jobs by the end of 2014.

2. He'd kill Medicare. He'd replace Medicare with vouchers for retirees to purchase insurance, eliminating the guarantee of health care for seniors and putting them at the mercy of the private insurance industry. That could amount to a cost increase of more than $5,900 by 2050, leaving many seniors broke or without the health care they need. He'd also raise the age of eligibility to 67.

3. He'd pickpocket the middle class to line the pockets of the rich. His tax plan is Robin Hood in reverse. He wants to cut taxes by $4.6 trillion over the next decade, but only for corporations and the rich, like giving families earning more than $1 million a year a $300,000 tax cut. And to pay for them, he'd raise taxes on middle- and lower-income households and butcher social service programs that help middle- and working-class Americans.

4. He's an anti-choice extremist. Ryan co-sponsored an extremist anti-choice bill, nicknamed the 'Let Women Die Act,' that would have allowed hospitals to deny women emergency abortion care even if their lives were at risk. And he co-sponsored another bill that would criminalize some forms of birth control, all abortions, and in vitro fertilization.

5. He'd dismantle Social Security. Ironically, Ryan used the Social Security Survivors benefit to help pay for college, but he wants to take that possibility away from future generations. He agrees with Rick Perry's view that Social Security is a "Ponzi scheme" and he supported George W. Bush's disastrous proposal to privatize Social Security.

6. He'd eliminate Pell grants for more than 1 million low-income students. His budget plan cuts the Pell Grant program by $200 billion, which could mean a loss of educational funding for 1 million low-income students.

7. He'd give $40 billion in subsidies to Big Oil. His budget includes oil tax breaks worth $40 billion, while cutting "billions of dollars from investments to develop alternative fuels and clean energy technologies that would serve as substitutes for oil."

8. He's another Koch-head politician. Not surprisingly, the billionaire oil-baron Koch brothers are some of Ryan's biggest political contributors. And their company, Koch industries, is Ryan's biggest energy-related donor. The company's PAC and affiliated individuals have given him $65,500 in donations.

9. He opposes gay rights. Ryan has an abysmal voting record on gay rights. He's voted to ban adoption by gay couples, against same-sex marriage, and against repealing "don't ask, don't tell." He also voted against the Hate Crimes Prevention Act, which President Obama signed into law in 2009.

10. He thinks an "I got mine, who cares if you're okay" philosophy is admirable. For many years, Paul Ryan devoted himself to Ayn Rand's philosophy of selfishness as a virtue. It has shaped his entire ethic about whom he serves in public office. He even went as far as making his interns read her work.

If there was ever any doubt that Mitt Romney's got a disastrous plan for America — he made himself 100% clear when he picked right-wing extremist Paul Ryan as his running mate. Paul Ryan is bad for America, but we can't beat him if Americans don't know everything he stands for.

Thank you Move on for the wonderful write up!

Now another thing people do not look at is who has Romney chosen to be his chief staff members and I will only list two and those two should scare everyone about the future and the vision they have.

First we start with John Bolton, who Romney wants to run our Foreign Policies: This man is a WAR HAWK and wants to attack IRAN as soon as Republicans take control of the country. I would call him nothing but Scary.

"The only other option is to take pre-emptive military action to break Iran's program, and the odds of doing so successfully are deteriorating daily, as it hardens and deeply buries new facilities."
John Bolton

John R. Bolton
From Wikipedia, the free encyclopedia

John Robert Bolton (born November 20, 1948) is an American lawyer and diplomat who has served in several Republican administrations. Appointed on a recess appointment, he served as the U.S. ambassador to the United Nations from August 2005 until December 2006. He resigned in December 2006, when the recess appointment would have otherwise ended, because he was unlikely to win senate confirmation.

Bolton is currently a senior fellow at the American Enterprise Institute (AEI), frequent op-ed contributor to the Wall Street Journal and the National Review, Fox News Channel commentator, and of counsel to the law firm Kirkland & Ellis, in their Washington D.C. office. He is also involved with a broad assortment of other conservative think tanks and policy institutes, including the Jewish Institute for National Security Affairs (JINSA), Project for the New American Century (PNAC), Institute of East-West Dynamics, National Rifle Association, U.S. Commission on International Religious Freedom, and the Council for National Policy (CNP). Known for his strong views on foreign policy, often equating diplomacy with weakness and indecisiveness, Bolton is often described as a neoconservative, though he personally rejects the term.

The Next guy we need to talk about is Robert Bork. Romney has selected this man to be the one to select Judges under a Romney President, here are a couple of quotes that should tell you all you need to know about this man and why Romney should never smell the White House.

"Robert Bork's America is a land in which women would be forced into back-alley abortions, blacks would sit at segregated lunch counters, rogue police could break down citizens' doors in midnight raids, school children could not

be taught about evolution, writers and artists could be censored at the whim of the Government, and the doors of the Federal courts would be shut on the fingers of millions of citizens for whom the judiciary is — and is often the only — protector of the individual rights that are the heart of our democracy ... President Reagan is still our president. But he should not be able to reach out from the muck of Irangate, reach into the muck of Watergate and impose his reactionary vision of the Constitution on the Supreme Court and the next generation of Americans. No justice would be better than this injustice."
Ted Kennedy was quoted from when they turned him down as a Supreme Court Justice

"Robert Bork is a right-wing ideologue. As a Supreme Court Justice, he would show little respect for the past 30 years of judicial precedent. Acting on dogmatic, narrow-minded views, he might vote to overrule landmark decisions on abortion, civil rights and church-state separation."
Time Magazine --- Before he was turned down as a Supreme Court Justice

BORK wants to set this country back so far there was no constitution or country.

Robert Bork :
1. Is opposed to Civil Rights.
2. Has indicated that there is no right to contraception, even within the confines of marriage.
3. Opposed to the recognition of the Right of Free Speech for anything except political philosophy, and has specifically opposed the notion that science is protected by the First Amendment.
4. Supportive of laws that attempt to control the identity of people with whom anyone can have sex.
5. Committed to the notion that the Constitution does NOT shield women from gender discrimination.

Four of the current Supreme Court Justices are over age 70. One of these justices is a cancer survivor. So whoever takes the oath of office in 2013 will likely have the opportunity to fill several of these seats. Now that Romney has selected Bork as one of his chief judicial advisers, all Americans should be focused on the fact that Robert Bork could determine the identity of the next several Supreme Court Justices.

There are three terrorist's organizations working in America to undermine and take control sending this country to a third world status under a Fascist type of government.

These three are ALEC, US Chamber of Commerce and Goldman Sachs (Wall Street.)

Quote from ALEC EXPOSED:

"Through the corporate-funded American Legislative Exchange Council, global corporations and state politicians vote behind closed doors to try to rewrite state laws that govern your rights."

"RIGHT TO WORK", "VOTER ID" and "TORT REFORM" include all your social issues and going after women can be traced to ALEC.

Sun Tzu (Chinese General and Author, b.500 BC)
"If you know the enemy and know yourself, your victory will not stand in doubt; if you know Heaven and know Earth, you may make your victory complete."

ALEC:
From Wikipedia, the free encyclopedia

ALEC is not a lobby; it is not a front group. It is much more powerful than that. Through ALEC, behind closed doors, corporations hand state legislators the changes to the law they desire that directly benefit their bottom line.

Along with legislators, corporations have membership in ALEC. Corporations sit on all nine ALEC task forces and vote with legislators to approve "model" bills. They have their own corporate governing board which meets jointly with the legislative board. (ALEC says that corporations do not vote on the board.) They fund almost all of Ale's operations.

Participating legislators, overwhelmingly conservative Republicans, then bring those proposals home and introduce them in state houses across the land as their own brilliant ideas and important public policy innovations — without disclosing that corporations crafted and voted on the bills.

ALEC boasts that it has over 1,000 of these bills introduced by legislative members every year, with one in every five of them enacted into law. ALEC describes itself as a "unique," "unparalleled" and "unmatched" organization. It might be right. It is as if a state legislature had been reconstituted, yet corporations had pushed the people out the door.

U.S. Chamber of Commerce:

This group is laundering money from all over the world (not proven but suspected) to fund the GOP SUPER PACS.

From Wikipedia, the free encyclopedia

This year numerous high-profile members quit the U.S. Chamber over its climate policy (Apple, Exelon, PG&E, PSEG, Levi Strauss & Co, the San Francisco Chamber of Commerce, and Mohawk Paper). Nike resigned from the chamber's Board of Directors, while Johnson & Johnson, General Electric, Alcoa, Duke, Entergy, Microsoft, and Royal Dutch Shell said the chamber doesn't represent their views on climate.

U.S. Chamber of Commerce, a powerful business lobbying group in the United States that "has become a fully functional part of the partisan Republican machine" since CEO and president Thomas J. Donohue took office in 1997. Prior to Donohue's tenure, the Chamber "used to be a trade association that advocated in a bipartisan manner for narrowly tailored policies to benefit its members." The Chamber's 2010 budget is approximately $200 million, but as a trade organization, its donors can remain anonymous.

The Chamber claims on its website that its mission is to "advance human progress through an economic, political and social system based on individual freedom, incentive, initiative, opportunity, and responsibility." It describes itself as "the world's largest business federation representing more than 3 million businesses and organizations of every size, sector, and region."

Despite these claims, the New York Times reported in October 2010 that half of the Chamber's $140 million in contributions in 2008 came from just 45 big-money donors, many of whom enlisted the Chamber's help to fight political and public opinion battles on their behalf (such as opposing financial or healthcare reforms, or other regulations).   The Chamber is "dominated by oil companies, pharmaceutical giants, automakers and other polluting industries," according to James Carter, executive director of the Green Chamber of Commerce.

Almost all things bad going on in this country can be trace back to these two groups.

WALL STREET:

Goldman Sachs and the rest of the Wall Street Banks are what I call the Number one terrorist group / organizations in the world.

Look to Greece and Europe and you will see the nasty works of Goldman Sachs. They are the ones forcing countries to do AUSTERITY which so far has been one disaster after another for the Countries that have done what told from these greedy criminals.

For those that do not know the economy tanked because of Wall Street and to date we have not seen one of them put in Jail (This is a priority wish of mine).

Time to bring back the Glass-Steagall Act and break up all the banks (another priority wish of mine).

Seems it might be a bit late because from all that I have read they have been doing all the things the brought the country down all over. Remember the Republicans want to give the Wall Street Criminals the 2.7 trillion dollar surplus that is currently in the Social Security Fund. Wonder how long before the entire fund is lost on Bonuses and Bad Investments.

Here is a quote from the movie Wall Street that is right on the money:

By: Gordon Gekko: WALL STREET MOVIE

"The richest one percent of this country owns half our country's wealth, five trillion dollars. One third of that comes from hard work, two thirds comes from inheritance, interest on interest accumulating to widows and idiot sons and what I do, stock and real estate speculation. It's bullshit. You got ninety percent of the American public out there with little or no net worth. I create nothing. I own. We make the rules, pal. The news, war, peace, famine, upheaval, the price per paper clip. We pick that rabbit out of the hat while everybody sits out there wondering how the hell we did it. Now you're not naive enough to think we're living in a democracy, are you buddy? It's the free market. And you're a part of it. You've got that killer instinct. Stick around pal, I've still got a lot to teach you."

Add in Koch Brothers and Blackwater and you have the makings of the American Nazi Party.

Note on Blackwater:
This organization, is a private right wing army trained and ready to take over state governments, by force if needed.
They are homing their skills in Michigan. Meaning all of us need to keep track of Michigan for this is what they will do to the country if they get total power.

Remember this the GOP tests things at the state level before taking it to the national level.

"Mussolini's path to power. They took over city governments first, then seized the municipal post offices (communication) and public transit (transportation). They attacked the Church and schools (social institutions), unions and all political opposition. Then they marched onto Rome and consolidated political power. They made war on Libya, Somalia and Ethiopia."

ALEC and the Chamber of Commerce backed with the money of the Koch Brothers and people like them are going all out in 2012 to end Democracy in America and install a Fascist Authoritarian Government.

Michigan's One-Man Rule: Even Worse Than the Rest of the Midwest
By Charles P. Pierce
"The governor of Michigan has been granted the power to suspend unilaterally the democratically elected government of any city based on criteria that he alone can determine. "

Fascism in Michigan By Josh Sager on 3/21/12
"Do we live in a country where our elected officials can appoint local dictators and nullify our votes in certain elections? No, we live in a constitutional republic, where voting is supposed to decide public representation. Dictatorship is un-American and cannot be tolerated no matter whether the dictator agrees with you or not.'

Remember what I am trying to do here is show you pattern's of how the right wing works and hopefully you can take it from there and investigate for yourself.

ALEC Exposed By Stephen D. Foster Jr.:

Twenty most dangerous men.

America has enemies. Not just abroad, but within our shores as well. And our domestic enemies, as it turns out, are MORE dangerous and destructive than the terrorists could ever hope to be. Because while the terrorists want to destroy us, the following people and their organizations are doing far more damage.

1. **Roger Ailes**: The President of Fox News keeps the right-wing mouth piece biased and unbalanced. He literally proposed a right-wing news network as a propaganda tool to use during the Nixon Administration. And now, Fox News makes every effort to slander Democrats, lie to the public, and support conservative groups, activists and politicians at all costs.

Want to tell Ailes what you think of him? Feel free to contact Fox News Channel by mail, phone, or email.

FOX News Channel
1211 Avenue of the Americas, 2nd Floor
New York, NY 10036
Phone: 212-301-3000
Web: www.foxnews.com

2. **The Koch Brothers:** Yes, there is more than one Koch brother, but rather than jotting down the same paragraph twice, it makes more sense to combine the two. Charles and David Koch are the owners of Koch Industries, a private oil and chemicals company. They have spent big money in elections and have pretty much bought and paid for all of Republicans that sit on the energy committee. They also have ties to The John Birch Society, of which their father was a founding member, and several other conservative think tanks and organizations including, Americans For Prosperity which David Koch leads as chairman, the Heritage Foundation, the American Legislative Exchange Council (ALEC), and the Cato Institute. They helped create and fund the Tea Party and have been very influential in the watering down of environmental laws and the destruction of unions. If you really want to see the scope of their influence look at what is happening in Wisconsin and in the U.S. House of Representatives.

I know you must be dying to contact Koch Industries to give them your opinion, so here's how you can do that.

Koch Industries, Inc.

P.O. Box 2256
Wichita, KS 67201-2256
Phone:316-828-5500
Fax:316-828-5739
info@kochind.com

3. **Dick Armey:** His Freedom Works organization helped to create the Tea Party and he has worked closely with the Koch brothers. Armey's organization seeks to deregulate and tear down reform. He opposed health care reform and is largely responsible for hatred, paranoia and anti-government sentiments displayed at town halls during the health care debate.

Freedom Works
400 North Capitol Street, NW, Suite 765
Washington, DC 20001
Toll Free Phone: 1-888-564-6273
Local Phone: 202-783-3870
Fax: 202-942-7649

4. **Tom Donohue:** The US Chamber Of Commerce President gained a hell of a lot more power in the wake of the Citizens United ruling. The Chamber is the largest conservative lobbying group in the country. Representing big corporations more than small businesses, the Chamber opposed health care reform and Wall Street reform. The group is in favor of tearing down any and every law designed to protect the American worker. Donohue once stated that "there are legitimate values in outsourcing — not only jobs, but work…." and once told unemployed people in Ohio to "stop whining". So, not only is he for deregulation, he supports job killing policies. That is a double dose of dangerous.

U.S. Chamber of Commerce
1615 H Street, NW
Washington, DC 20062-2000
Main Number: 202-659-6000
Phone: 1-800-638-6582

5. **Tony Perkins:** Perkins is the President of the Family Research Council, a hate group according to the Southern Poverty Law Center. The Council opposes abortion for any reason, believes homosexuality should be against the law, believes in teaching "intelligent design" in schools, and believes global warming is a hoax. FRC was listed as a hate group after it falsely linked gay males to pedophilia. It basically lobbies the government to make laws that govern our personal and private lives. The Council is a Christian Right-wing organization

that has a heavy influence on the Republican Party, hence all the abortion laws being proposed by them.

Family Research Council
801 G Street, NW
Washington DC 20001
Phone: 1-800-225-4008

6. **Pat Robertson:** Robertson founded the Christian Coalition in 1989 and claims to be non-partisan. The problem with this claim is that it's a bunch of crap. The Christian Coalition passes out "voter guides" in churches and yet is granted tax exempt status. It clearly supports a conservative agenda and is associated with Christian fundamentalism. It is yet another group that believes that America should be a Christian state. They are a threat to the Constitution.

Christian Coalition of America
PO Box 37030
Washington, DC 20013-7030
Phone: 202-479-6900

7. **Edwin Feulner, Jr.**: Feulner is the President of the Heritage Foundation, a conservative think tank that took a leading role in the conservative movement during the 1980's and continues to push conservative ideals today. The Foundation has strong ties to many Republican politicians, and many Heritage personnel members have gone on to serve in senior governmental roles. Not only does it stand by supply side economics and tax cuts for the rich and corporations which led to the current economic crisis, it also believes in a strong defense which has become more and more expensive. Heritage Foundation is also a part of the Koch Foundation Associate Program and is perhaps the most powerful public policy think tank on this list. Supreme Court Justice Clarence Thomas has taken money from the organization. It has far too much influence on American policy and that influence must be brought to an end.

The Heritage Foundation
214 Massachusetts Ave NE
Washington DC 20002-4999
Phone: 202-546-4400

8. **Arthur Thompson:** Thompson leads the radical right-wing John Birch Society, which is yet another organization that has Koch family connections. Founded in 1958 by Robert Welch, Jr., the John Birch Society is an anti-communism group that has pretty much denounced every liberal person and policy as socialist. It opposes the Civil Rights Act, the United Nations, and believes in immigration

reduction. It aims to dismantle the Federal Reserve System and wants to return to the gold standard. The group is a sponsor of CPAC and is no longer exiled from the mainstream. Another interesting fact is that Fred Koch, father of the aforementioned Koch brothers, was a founding member.

John Birch Society
770 N. West hill Blvd
Appleton, Wisconsin 54914
Phone: 920-749-3780

9. **Rupert Murdoch:** Known as "the man who owns the news", Murdoch controls a vast media empire around the world including Fox News, The New York Post, and the Wall Street Journal here in America. Advertising his media outlets as "fair and balanced" Murdoch and his News Corporation relentlessly push conservative talking points and provide campaign donations to many Republicans running for various positions. News Corporation now has to answer for hacking cell phones and impeding investigations. Long the mouthpiece for Republican propaganda, Murdoch is a threat to Freedom of the Press and the foundations that keep America free.

If you want to contact News Corporation and tell them what you think of them, here is their contact information.

News Corporation
1211 Avenue of Americas
New York, New York 10036
Phone: 212-852-7000
Web: www.newscorp.com

10. **Grover Norquist:** Norquist is an especially dangerous individual. In fact, at the moment, he has the most influence on Republican congressmen. Republicans in the House and Senate refuse to raise taxes on corporations and the wealthy and Norquist and his group, Americans For Tax Reform, have made sure Republicans continue to do so. 235 members of the House and 41 Senators signed the Norquist pledge to not raise taxes and now our economic future hangs in the balance. Norquist is basically calling the shots and holding America hostage on behalf of the rich. And he isn't even an elected official.

More on Grover Norquist:
Grover Norquist, Wikipedia
Daily Kos: In his own non-words: Grover Norquist is a plutocrat
Norquist history 101

Americans for Tax Reform
722 12th Street, NW
Fourth Floor
Washington, DC 20005
Office: 202-785-0266
Fax: 202-785-026

11. **David Bossie:** Citizens United isn't just a bad Supreme Court ruling. Citizens United is the conservative organization that the conservative majority of the Supreme Court ruled in favor of in 2008. Founded in 1988, located near Capitol Hill, and led by President and Chairman David Bossie, Citizens United's goals include withdrawal from the United Nations, and defeat of campaign finance laws, among others. They also produce "documentaries" that serve the conservative agenda. The group is mostly a threat because of their fight to allow corporate ownership of elections. The Koch brothers, and many conservative think tanks and organizations have flooded elections with cash since the ruling. The Supreme Court decision alone is enough to put this dangerous organization and Bossie on the list.

Citizens United
1006 Pennsylvania Ave SE
Washington, DC 20003
Office: (202) 547-5420
Fax: (202) 547-5421

12. **Tim LaHaye and Kenneth Cribb:** Once again, you'll notice that two people occupy this spot. After some thought, I decided this was necessary to avoid repetition. Tim Lahaye founded, and Kenneth Cribb is the current President of, the Council for National Policy. The CNP is a conservative organization for social conservative activists. Described by The New York Times as a "little-known group of a few hundred of the most powerful conservatives in the country," the organization is perhaps the most powerful group on this list. Members include many who are already on this list such as James Dobson, Pat Robertson, Tony Perkins, Phyllis Schlafly, and Edwin Feulner Jr. What makes this group particularly dangerous is that they support theocracy and Dominionism as national policy. They are also incredibly secretive and that's scary all by itself.

CNP is apparently so secret that no address or phone number is available, so you'll have to email them.
info@cfnp.org
Website: http://www.cfnp.org/

13. **Steven J. Law:** Lawis President and CEO of American Crossroads, a conservative organization that has raised and spent tens of millions of dollars to defend and elect Republican candidates to federal office, and was very active in the 2010 U.S. midterm elections. Basically, Law and his group are listed because they have taken advantage of the Citizens United Supreme Court decision the most since the ruling. The Koch's and Karl Rove have connections with the group and are a major reason why the House is under GOP control.

American Crossroads
P.O. Box 34413
Washington, DC 20043
Phone: (202) 559-6428.
info@americancrossroads.org

14. **James Dobson:** Dobson is the Family Talk radio personality and Family Research Council founder that contributes greatly to all the hate we see from conservatives. A frequent guest on Fox News, he is perhaps the most influential religious leader on the Christian-Right even though he has never been ordained. Dobson believes that women should only focus on mothering (and probably cooking too) and is totally against gay rights. He supports private schools and special tax privileges for religious schools. He opposes sex education and only supports abstinence as the only technique for pregnancy prevention. Dobson is on this list because he is the one that began all of the anti-gay, anti-women, and anti-education speeches that are now commonplace in the Republican Party. [Note from The Christian Left: This is the saddest entry for us. Some of us used to really enjoy James Dobson. It's unfortunate that he joined the extreme right. Maybe he'll see the light some day.]

Family Talk Radio
540 Elkton Drive
Suite 201
Colorado Springs, CO 80907
Phone: 877-732-6825

15. **Phyllis Schally:** She is the only woman on this list. Undoubtedly, you may have thought that Michele Bachmann or Sarah Palin would be, but they are not. I consider Palin and Bachmann mere pawns compared to Schlafly. As founder and President of the Eagle Forum, Schlafly opposes feminism and equal rights for women. Eagle Forum promotes a pro-life, anti-gay, anti-sex education, and anti-vaccination agenda that has contributed to the current wave of social conservative extremism in the Republican Party. She believes women should remain in the home and that there is no such things as marital rape. She is

certainly the most influential woman in right-wing activism and as such, the most dangerous one too.

Eagle Forum
PO Box 618
Alton, IL 62002
Phone: 618-462-5415
Fax: 618-462-8909
eagle@eagleforum.org

16. **David Keene:** Up to now David Keene led the American Conservative Union, which is the oldest operating conservative lobbying organization in the country. The ACU runs the event known as CPAC and spends money on lobbying and political campaigns. Keene is still the current President of the National Rifle Association. Which is also a strong lobbying group that is virtually an arm of the Republican Party that glorifies guns and believes that people should be able to carry guns anywhere they go, even near the President of the United States. Keene is mostly on this list because of the NRA. The NRA used to actually serve a valid purpose but has since become a pro-Republican political organization that has mixed guns and politics. It makes them a danger to the political process.

The American Conservative Union
1007 Cameron Street
Alexandria, VA 22314
Phone: 703-836-8602
Fax: 703-836-8606

National Rifle Association of America
11250 Waples Mill Road
Fairfax, VA 22030
Phone: 1-800-672-3888

17. **Tim Wildmon:** Classified as a hate group by the Southern Poverty Law Center, the American Family Association is headed by Tim Wildmon. AFA is just like every other conservative Christian group. It opposes abortion and gay rights, as well as other public policy goals such as deregulation of the oil industry and lobbying against the Employee Free Choice Act. The group has actively boycotted just about any business that disagrees with them. In the wake of the Virginia Tech shootings, the AFA released a video in which "God" tells a student that students were killed in schools because God isn't allowed in schools anymore and blamed the shootings on abortion and lack of prayer in schools. AFA is against all other religions and has an obsession with Christmas, often boycotting companies that do not mention Christmas in their advertising. AFA is

here on this list because they represent one of the biggest threats to intellectual and personal freedom in America.

Want to boycott AFA? Send them a "friendly" letter.

American Family Association
P.O. Box 3206
Tupelo, MS 38803

18. **David Barton:** Despite not having any history or law credentials David Barton passes himself off as an expert in early American history. Most of his claims have been disputed and written off as false by real historians. Barton's organization is Wallbuilders, which seeks to destroy one the basic foundations of American life: the separation of church and state. Barton's mission is to revise history in an effort to turn America into a Christian state with Biblical law instituted as the law of the land. He has also created false quotes to justify his claims. Barton is a danger to the history of America, the Constitution, and education.

WallBuilders
PO Box 397
Aledo, TX 76008
Phone: 817-441-6044

19. **Noble Ellington:** American Legislative Exchange Council, also known as ALEC. The Council is basically a pay to play organization that carries the corporate agenda into state legislatures across the country. They work to end unions, end environmental and labor regulations, and end consumer protection laws. ALEC has been funded by the Koch brothers for two decades. The price for corporate participation is an ALEC membership fee of as much as $25,000. For that price, corporations are basically writing the legislation that you are currently seeing being proposed and implemented in Republican controlled states across the country.

American Legislative Exchange Council
1101 Vermont Ave. N.W., 11th Floor
Washington, D.C. 20005
Phone: 202-466-3800
Fax: 202-466-3801

20. **Edward H. Crane:** Crane is the founder and current leader of the Cato Institute. While they have supported some liberal policies and claim to abhor neo-conservatives, the Cato Institute does push many objectives that should make everyone cringe. Among the various policies that Cato supports, privatizing Social Security, abolishing the minimum wage, abolishing affirmative action, and some environmental regulations, are among them. Of course, it's understandable why Cato holds these positions considering Charles Koch is chairman of the board and a major funding source. Even Rupert Murdoch had a place on the board at one point which connects the Koch's and the right-wing media.

Cato Institute
1000 Massachusetts Avenue, N.W.
Washington D.C. 20001-5403
Phone: 202-842-0200
Fax: 202-842-3490

And there you have it. All of these people and their organizations pose a serious threat to the American people. They target women, senior citizens, minorities, homosexuals, non-Christians, and American workers.

So which person or organization is the most dangerous to democracy? The common thread throughout the list is the Koch brothers. They have ties to many of the people and organizations on the list and share many of the same goals. If one were to remove the Koch brothers from the equation an important source of funding and leadership would be eliminated from the conservative sphere.

The Koch brothers are by far the biggest threat to American values and institutions. The truly evil thing about this group is that NONE of them are elected by the people. Yet they have more power and influence over our elected officials and system of law and government, than we do.

Edited By: Alexis Atherton

Stephen Foster holds a Bachelor's Degree in History and Political Science from Missouri University of Science and Technology. He is a certified teacher in Pennsylvania and Missouri and enjoys performing historical research, debating, and writing. He lives in Missouri.

Article used by permission under Creative Commons License

Here are a Few left out that need to be added for reference:

Paul Singer
U.S. Chamber of Commerce board member.

William Walton
Allied Capital CEO

Peter Peterson
The thing about Wall Streeters is that no matter how much money you give them, they always want more. Now they are using their political power and control over the media to attack Social Security. This effort is being led by billionaire investment banker Peter Peterson.

Old-line anti-communists from the Cuban-American community including **Otto Reich** and CIA propagandist **Walter Raymond Jr.**

Gregory Boyce, Peabody Coal CEO
Along with his Board and shareholders, surely one of the most malignant men of the 21st century. Boyce's mission in life is to see that the world burns as much coal as possible, in spite of scientists' warnings that this path is already heating the planet and destroying life. Pays lobbyists to fight regulation of coal plants' emissions of cancer-causing mercury, sulfur dioxide, and nitrous oxide.

Tony Hayward, former BP CEO
Prior to the Deepwater Horizon explosion, he presided over furious maintenance and safety cost cutting efforts, leading to higher profits, despite internal warnings. "Managed" the expanding oil plumes by claiming that only 1,000 barrels a day were escaping, later modified to 5,000 barrels a day. Hayward was perfectly aware that the actual figure was closer to 50,000 barrels.

David Lesar, Halliburton CEO
Oversees a company whose missions are to bribe politicians, screw taxpayers, and subcontract work to the lowest, most incompetent bidder. Faulty work by subsidiary KBR in Iraq led to the electrocution of US soldiers while they were taking showers. Charged $45 a case for Coca Cola in Iraq and $100 for a load of laundry. Halliburton knowingly used faulty cement on the Deepwater Horizon, which was a major cause of the explosion, but such is their juice in DC that even Obama is still handing them no bid contracts, even though they moved their headquarters to Dubai.

Phil Anschutz, who owns the Washington Examiner.
Major GOP donor

The DeVos Family:
Meet the Super-Wealthy Right-wingers Working With the Religious Right to Kill Public Education

Clearly, it's had an effect over 30 odd years. Clearly, there are a lot of hateful people who call themselves Christian.

"Shake the dust from your feet."

"When People who are in the Public Eye and profess to be Christian but do not believe in taking care of the Poor, Sick and Elderly or to live by the Golden Rule, these people are truly Charlatans"
Jeff Carlson

President Barrack Obama

All we hear is that Obama, did not do this and he did not do that, but what he has done is remarkable considering he has had the Republican party blocking all efforts to moving this country forward at a faster pace.

We now have seen 30 + months of job growth and we have replaced the jobs lost under the Bush Admin. We have seen the stock market go from 6000+ to 13000+

I do not always agree with President Obama, but I respect what he has had to overcome after 8 years of a Bush Administration that tore apart the middle class and almost caused a major depression.

"The important work of moving the world forward does not wait to be done by perfect men."
By: George Eliot (1819 – 1880 one of the leading female English novelists of the 19th century.)

"Why do we asked Obama to be perfect, he is doing the important work of the world and is moving us along while having to deal with hatred at all levels and the GOP that wants to destroy him. I say Obama you have done a remarkable job and let us watch your back."
By: Jeff Carlson.

"To practice five things under all circumstances constitutes perfect virtue; these five are gravity, generosity of soul, sincerity, earnestness, and kindness."
By: Confucius

I love the quote from Confucius because you can see in Obama those virtues. Those who hate him because he is not white will never see any virtues because of blindness from the hate they carry for him and all Non Caucasians.

Here is a great article put together by: "The PCTC Blog: Common Sense Progressive Politics"

What has Obama Done? Here Are 194 Accomplishments! With Citations!

If you're one of those who thinks President Obama is a "disappointment," my condolences for not getting your unicorn. And it's time to grow up, get over it. We have four months to go before an election that will feature more political ads than you have ever seen before in your life. We're not just having to beat Willard Romney; we also have to beat Citizens United. There will be TWO choices for president. You can either work for Obama and every other Democrat (yes, including Blue Dogs), or you can sit back and watch Willard Romney complete the job of taking apart the social fabric of the country that was begun by Ronald Reagan.

What makes the "disappointment" argument even more irritating is that it's simply not true. He's done nearly everything we elect a president to do, and he did it all with little support from the left, and massive obstruction from the right.

Is he perfect? No, he's human. Does he deserve some criticism? At this point, it really doesn't matter.

What does matter is that this president has compiled a STELLAR record. If you can look at this list of the president's accomplishments after three years, and not be excited, you have a serious problem with perspective.

Pass this list around to everyone you know. And don't be afraid; unlike many such lists, every item includes a link to a citation supporting it.

He Returned the Executive Branch to Fiscal Responsibility After the Bush Debacle

1. Within his first week, he signed an Executive Order ordering an audit of government contracts, and combating waste and abuse. http://1.usa.gov/dUvbu5

2. Created the post of Chief Performance Officer, whose job it is to make operations more efficient to save the federal government money. http://n.pr/hcgBn1

3. On his first full day, he froze White House salaries. http://on.msnbc.com/ewJUIx

4. He appointed the first Federal Chief Information Officer to oversee federal IT spending. http://www.cio.gov

5. He committed to phasing out unnecessary and outdated weapons systems. To that end, he also signed the Democratic-sponsored Weapons Systems Acquisition Reform Act, which attempted to put a stop to waste, fraud and abuse in the

defense procurement and contracting system. http://bit.ly/hOw1t1
http://bit.ly/fz8GAd

6. Through an executive order, he created the National Commission on Fiscal Responsibility and Reform. http://bit.ly/hwKhKa

He Improved the Economy, Preventing a Bush Depression

7. Pushed through and signed the Democratic-sponsored American Recovery and Reinvestment Act, otherwise known as "the stimulus package." The bill passed, even though only three Republicans voted for it. In a major departure from the previous administration, he launched recovery.gov, a website that allows taxpayers to track spending from the Act. http://1.usa.gov/ibiFSs
http://1.usa.gov/e3BJMk

8. The Bush-led Great Recession was costing the economy nearly 800,000 jobs per month by the time President Obama took office. But by the end of his first year, the American Recovery and Reinvestment Act created and sustained 2.1 million jobs and stimulated the economy by 3.5%. http://reut.rs/i46CEE

9. Not only did he completed the massive TARP financial and banking rescue plan, he also leaned on the banks and others, and recovered virtually all of the bail-out money. http://1.usa.gov/eA5jVS   http://bit.ly/eCNrD6

10. He created the Making Home Affordable home refinancing plan. http://1.usa.gov/goy6zl

11. Oversaw the creation of more jobs in 2010 alone than Bush did in eight years. http://bit.ly/hrrnjY

12. Along with Democrats, and almost no Republicans, implemented an auto industry rescue plan, and saved as many as 1 million jobs. http://bit.ly/ibhpxr Many are of the opinion that he saved the entire auto industry, and even the economy of the entire Midwest. http://bit.ly/gj7mt5 This resulted in GM returning to its place as the top car company in the world. http://lat.ms/zIJuQx Willard Romney, on the other hand, advocated for the entire industry to go belly-up. http://nyti.ms/k0zp

13. Doubled funding for the Manufacturing Extension Partnership, which is designed to improve manufacturing efficiency. http://bit.ly/eYD4nf

14. Signed the Democratic-sponsored Fraud Enforcement and Recovery Act giving the federal government more tools to investigate and prosecute fraud in

every corner of the financial system, and create a bipartisan Financial Crisis Inquiry Commission to investigate the financial fraud that led to the economic meltdown. http://abcn.ws/g18Fe7

15. Signed the Democratic-sponsored Credit Card Accountability, Responsibility and Disclosure (CARD) Act, which was designed to protect consumers from unfair and deceptive credit card practices. http://1.usa.gov/glaNcS

16. Increased infrastructure spending after years of neglect. http://bit.ly/f77aOw

17. Signed the Democratic-sponsored and passed Helping Families Save Their Homes Act, expanding on the Making Home Affordable Program to help millions of Americans avoid preventable foreclosures. The bill also provided $2.2 billion to help combat homelessness, and to stabilize the housing market. http://bit.ly/eEpLFn

18. Through the Worker, Homeownership, and Business Assistance Act of 2009, he and Congressional Democrats provided tax credits to first-time home buyers, which helped the U.S. housing market recovery. http://bit.ly/dZgXXw http://bit.ly/gORYfL

19. Initiated a $15 billion plan designed to encourage increased lending to small businesses.
http://1.usa.gov/eu0u0b

20. Created business.gov, which allows for online collaboration between small businesses and experts re managing a business. (The program has since merged with SBA.gov.) http://www.business.gov

21. Played a lead role in getting the G-20 Summit to commit to a $1.1 trillion deal to combat the global financial crisis. http://nyti.ms/gHlgp5

22. Took steps to improve minority access to capital. http://bit.ly/f9xVE7

23. Signed an Executive Order instructing federal agencies to review all federal regulations and remove any unnecessary and/or burdensome regulations from the books. http://1.usa.gov/Lpo5bd

24. Through the American Recovery and Reinvestment Act, saved at least 300,000 education jobs, such as teachers, principals, librarians, and counselors that would have otherwise been lost. http://1.usa.gov/ez30Dc

25. Dismantled the Minerals Management Service, thereby cutting ties between energy companies and the government. http://nyti.ms/bw1MLu

26. Along with Congressional Democrats, provided funding to states and the Department of Homeland Security to save thousands of police and firefighter jobs from being cut during the recession. http://bit.ly/g0IKWR

27. Used recovered TARP money to fund programs at local housing finance agencies in California, Florida, Nevada, Arizona and Michigan. http://on.msnbc.com/i1i8eV

28. Crafted an Executive order establishing the President's Advisory Council on Financial Capability to assist in financial education for all Americans. http://bit.ly/eyqsNE

He Fostered Greater Transparency and Better Government, After the Excesses of the Bush Years

29. Signed an order banning gifts from lobbyists to anyone in the Executive Branch. http://bit.ly/fsBACN

30. Signed an order banning anyone from working in an agency they had lobbied in previous years, and put strict limits on lobbyists' access to the White House. http://nyti.ms/gOrznV

31. Held the first-ever first online town hall from the White House, and took questions from the public. http://bit.ly/gVNSgX

32. Became the first to stream every White House event, live. http://1.usa.gov/kAgOP5

33. Established a central portal for Americans to find service opportunities. http://www.serve.gov

34. Provided the first voluntary disclosure of the White House Visitors Log in history. http://1.usa.gov/hQ7ttV

35. Issued an Executive Order on Presidential Records, which restored the 30-day time frame for former presidents to review records, and eliminated the right for the vice president or family members of former presidents to do the reviews. Provides the public with greater access for historic White House documents, and

severely curtails the ability to use executive privilege to shield them. http://1.usa.gov/gUetLb

36. Improved aspects of the Freedom of Information Act, and issued new guidelines to make FOIA more open and transparent when processing FOIA requests. http://1.usa.gov/gjrnp2

Wall Street Reforms and Consumer Protection

37. Ordered 65 executives who took bailout money to cut their own pay until they paid back all bailout money. http://huff.to/eAi9Qq

38. Along with Congressional Democrats, pushed through and got passed Dodd-Frank, one of the largest and most comprehensive Wall Street reforms since the Great Depression. http://bit.ly/hWCPg0 http://bit.ly/geHpcD

39. Through Dodd-Frank legislation, created the Consumer Financial Protection Bureau http://1.usa.gov/j5onG

40. Through Dodd-Frank, the Executive Branch fashioned rules that reduce the influence of speculators in the oil market. http://bit.ly/MDnA1t

41. Fashioned rules so that banks can no longer use YOUR money to invest in high-risk financial instruments that work against their own customers' interests. http://bit.ly/fnTayj

42. Supported the concept of allowing stockholders to vote on executive compensation. http://bit.ly/fnTayj

43. Endorsed and supported the Foreign Account Tax Compliance Act of 2009 that would close offshore tax avoidance loopholes. http://bit.ly/esOdfB http://bit.ly/eG4DPM

44. Negotiated a deal with Swiss banks that now permits the US government to gain access to the records of criminals and tax evaders. http://bit.ly/htfDgw

45. Signed the American Jobs and Closing Tax Loopholes Act, which closed many of the loopholes that allowed companies to send jobs overseas, and avoid paying US taxes by moving money offshore. http://1.usa.gov/bd1RTq

46. Established a Consumer Protection Financial Bureau designed to protect consumers from financial sector excesses. http://bit.ly/fnTayj

47. Oversaw and then signed a Democratic bill constituting the most sweeping food safety legislation since the Great Depression. http://thedc.com/gxkCtP

48. Through the Fraud Enforcement and Recovery Act, extended the False Claims Act to combat fraud by companies and individuals using money from the TARP and Stimulus programs. http://bit.ly/SLTcSa

He Ushered through Many Changes That Enhanced Civil Rights and Anti-Discrimination

49. Along with Congressional Democrats, advocated for and signed the Matthew Sheppard and James Byrd, Jr. Hate Crimes Prevention Act, which made it a federal crime to assault anyone based on his or her sexual orientation or gender identity. http://bit.ly/gsMSJ7

50. Pushed through, signed and demanded the Pentagon enact a repeal of the discriminatory "Don't Ask Don't Tell" policy that forced soldiers to lie in order to be eligible to fight for their country, and put our troops at risk by disqualifying many qualified soldiers from helping. http://bit.ly/fdahuH http://bit.ly/mZV4Pz

51. Extended benefits to same-sex partners of federal employees. http://1.usa.gov/g2RLCj

52. Appointed more openly gay officials than anyone in history. http://bit.ly/g1lA7D

53. Appointed first openly transgender Cabinet Official in History. http://bit.ly/58zUp7

54. Changed HUD rules to prohibit gender and sexual orientation-based discrimination in housing bit.ly/9RxEnP

55. Changed his mind and publicly expressed support for the right to enter into a same-sex marriage. http://bit.ly/JsiFKp

56. Issued a Presidential Memorandum reaffirming the rights of gay couples to make medical decisions for each other. http://1.usa.gov/aUueGT

57. Wrote and signed an Executive Order establishing a White House Council on Women and Girls to ensure that all Cabinet and Cabinet-level agencies evaluate

the effect of their policies and programs on women and families.
http://bit.ly/e1puTk   http://1.usa.gov/rFfqMM

58. Signed the Democratic-sponsored Lilly Ledbetter Fair Pay Act, which restored basic protections against pay discrimination for women and other workers. This was after the GOP blocked the bill in 2007. Only 5 Republican Senators voted for the bill.   http://bit.ly/fT3Cxg

59. Expanded funding for the Violence Against Women Act. http://1.usa.gov/dSbl0x

60. Under his guidance, National Labor Relations Board issued final rules that require all employers to prominently post employees' rights where all employees or prospective employees can see it, including websites and intranets, beginning November 2011. http://1.usa.gov/qu2EhQ

61. Advocated that United Nations adopt a policy supporting gay rights worldwide. http://lat.ms/pQe1RS

62. Issued an order requiring hospitals to allow visitation by same-sex couples. reut.rs/lINJek

63. Appointed Kareem Dale as the first ever Special Assistant to the President for Disability Policy. http://1.usa.gov/fi5IY0

64. Helped Democrats in Congress pass and signed the Civil Rights History Act. http://bit.ly/th0JC8

He Made Major Improvements in Foreign Relations and American Status around the World

65. Visited more countries and met with more world leaders than any previous president during his first six months in office.   http://bit.ly/hZycda

66. As he promised, he gave a speech at a major Islamic forum in Cairo early in his administration. http://nyti.ms/dKvY4g

67. Helped to restore America's reputation around the world as a global leader that does the "right thing" in world affairs, at least according to the rest of the world. http://bit.ly/h743y7 http://bit.ly/ho4TCr

68. Re-established and reinforced our partnership with NATO and other allies on strategic international issues. http://1.usa.gov/e7QuDj

69. Closed a number of secret detention facilities. http://nyti.ms/rpUc9l

70. Improved relations with Middle East countries by appointing special envoys. http://1.usa.gov/tiGAGe

71. Pushed for military to emphasize development of foreign language skills. http://bit.ly/AxUCLV

72. Offered $400 million to the people living in Gaza, called on both Israel and the Palestinians to stop inciting violence. http://bit.ly/9axfWh

73. Refused to give Israel the green light to attack Iran over their possible nuclear program, and thus avoid another war that Republicans wanted. http://bit.ly/xVmSZK

74. Worked with Democratic Congress to make donations to Haiti tax deductible in 2009. http://huff.to/6YkAVY

75. Established a new U.S.-China Strategic and Economic Dialogue. http://1.usa.gov/eX28DP

76. Issued Executive Order blocking interference and helping to stabilize Somalia. http://1.usa.gov/hxdf8U

77. Established new, more reasonable policies in our relations with Cuba, such as allowing Cuban-Americans to visit their families and send money to support them. http://n.pr/hY3Kwa http://nyti.ms/emQBde

78. Ordered the closure of the prison at Guantanamo Bay. It was Republicans (and, unfortunately, progressive Democrats) who prevented follow through. http://bit.ly/eW6CVF

79. Ordered a review of our detention and interrogation policy, and prohibited the use of torture, or what Bush called "enhanced interrogation." He ordered interrogators to limit their actions to the Army Field manual. http://bit.ly/g6MTuC

80. Ordered all secret detention facilities in Eastern Europe and elsewhere to be closed. http://bbc.in/h6N9ax

81. Released the Bush torture memos. http://bit.ly/hWJ5z0

82. On his second day in office, he signed a detailed Executive Order that banned torture, reversed all Bush torture policies, and put the United States in compliance with the Geneva Convention. http://1.usa.gov/dL6Zve http://nyti.ms/hzWWys

83. In response to the emerging "Arab Spring," he created a Rapid Response fund, to assist emerging democracies with foreign aid, debt relief, technical assistance and investment packages in order to show that the United States stands with them. http://bit.ly/zfmGv9

84. Passed the Iran Sanctions Act, to prevent war, and to encourage Iran to give up their nuclear program. http://1.usa.gov/wLtNjb

85. Ended the Iraq War. http://tgr.ph/ru0tyS

86. Authorized and oversaw a secret mission by SEAL Team Six to rescue two hostages held by Somali pirates. http://bit.ly/y8c9Fz

He Took a More Realistic Approach to "Defense"

87. Created a comprehensive new strategy for dealing with the international nuclear threat. http://1.usa.gov/gDX1nE

88. Authorized a $1.4 billion reduction in Star Wars program in 2010. http://1.usa.gov/gLFZl2

89. Restarted nuclear nonproliferation talks and built up the nuclear inspection infrastructure/protocols to where they had been before Bush. http://lat.ms/gkcl3i

90. Signed and pushed through ratification a new SALT Treaty. http://bit.ly/f3JVtw

91. Negotiated and signed a new START Treaty that will lst until at least 2021. http://1.usa.gov/cl1bC4

92. Through the Defense Authorization Act, reversed the Bush Administration and committed to no permanent military bases in Iraq. http://bit.ly/hk73OJ

93. Developed first comprehensive strategy with regard to Afghanistan and Pakistan designed to facilitate the defeat of al Qaeda and the withdrawal of most troops, as well as the rebuilding of Afghanistan. http://wapo.st/ee4Xcs

94. Returned our focus to Afghanistan, stabilized the country, and began the process of withdrawing our troops from the country. http://bit.ly/INXUna

95. Negotiated a deal with Afghan government, to withdraw troops and military support, while assisting in rebuilding and modernizing of the country. http://bit.ly/K362an

96. Took steps to severely weaken al Qaeda and limited their ability to terrorize the world. http://yhoo.it/n5lXs6

97. Negotiated and signed a nuclear nonproliferation treaty with India. http://1.usa.gov/aHp0Cn

98. Took decisive action to use NATO to limit the slaughter of innocents in Libya, so that the Libyan people could topple a despotic government and determine their own fate. http://aje.me/qAh4Sj

His Administration Treated Soldiers and Veterans with Respect That Was Missing Previously

99. Along with Congressional Democrats, not only reauthorized families of fallen soldiers to be able to visit when the body arrives at Dover AFB, but also provided funding for it. Ended the media blackout on coverage of the return of fallen soldiers. http://nyti.ms/glqN66 http://bbc.in/gWSSkA

100. Funded Department of Veterans Affairs (VA) with an extra $1.4 billion to improve veterans' services. http://1.usa.gov/huhqfo

101. Provided active combat troops with better body armor. http://bit.ly/hzSv2h

102. Created Joint Virtual Lifetime Electronic Record program for military personnel, in order to improve the quality of their medical care. http://1.usa.gov/f4yaxW

103. Put an end to the Bush-era stop-loss policy that kept soldiers in Iraq/Afghanistan beyond their enlistment date. (personal note: my son will be in harm's way for six fewer months with Obama as president, so you know I love this one.) http://nyti.ms/e2YQ7Q

104. Along with Congressional Democrats, supported and signed Veterans Health Care Budget Reform and Transparency Act, which made more money available to enable better medical care for veterans. http://1.usa.gov/fN4ur1

105. Along with Congressional Democrats, ushered through largest spending increase in 30 years for Department of Veterans Affairs, with money to go to improved medical facilities, and to assist states in acquiring or constructing state nursing homes and extended care facilities.   http://1.usa.gov/gY8O3x

106. Created the Green Vet Initiative, which provided special funding to the Labor Department to provide veterans with training in green jobs. http://bit.ly/epwUQY

107. Initiated and signed a recruitment and employment plan to get more veterans into government jobs. http://bit.ly/b48coi

108. Oversaw a $4.6 billion expansion of the Veterans Administration budget to pay for more mental health professionals. http://bit.ly/gjzTxX

109. Signed the Military Spouses Residency Relief Act, which ensures that spouses of military personnel who are forced to move because their spouse is posted for military duty will be able to avoid state taxes in their temporary residence. http://bit.ly/1Gh0NX

He Refocused the Federal Government on Education

110. Repeatedly increased funding for student financial aid, and at the same time cut the banks completely out of the process. http://bit.ly/gYWd30   http://bit.ly/e9c7Dr   http://bit.ly/eEzTNq

111. Reformed student loan program, to make it possible for students to refinance at a lower rate. http://nyti.ms/dMvHOt

112. Through the American Recovery and Reinvestment Act , invested heavily in elementary, secondary and post-secondary education. http://1.usa.gov/gGRIAr

113. Created the Race to the Top program, which encouraged states to come up with effective school reforms and rewards the best of them. http://bit.ly/NHtZ7L

114. Oversaw major expansion of broadband availability in K-12 schools nationwide   http://bit.ly/fNDcj3 ,

115. Oversaw major expansion in school construction. http://bit.ly/fYwNrV

116. Also through the American Recovery and Reinvestment Act, he put $5 billion into early education, including Head Start. http://1.usa.gov/tzT2Rr

117. Signed the Democratic-sponsored Post-9/11 GI Bill, also known as GI Bill 2.0 http://bit.ly/hPhG7J

118. Oversaw expansion of the Pell Grants program, to expand opportunity for low income students to go to college. http://bit.ly/hI6tXz

119. Along with Democratic Congress, passed and signed Individuals with Disabilities Education Act, which provided an extra $12.2 billion in funds. http://1.usa.gov/dQvtUe

He Pushed Through Improvements in National Safety and Security

120. Restored federal agencies such as FEMA to the point that they have been able to manage a huge number of natural disasters successfully. http://bit.ly/h8Xj7z

121. Authorized Navy SEALS to successfully secure the release of a US captain held by Somali pirates and increased patrols off the Somali coast. http://nyti.ms/efBO7B

122. Has repeatedly beefed up border security http://bit.ly/mMYB4i

123. Ordered and oversaw the Navy SEALS operation that killed Osama bin Laden. http://bit.ly/jChpgw

Science, Technology and Health Care

124. Created a Presidential Memorandum to restore scientific integrity in government decision-making. http://1.usa.gov/g2SDuw

125. Opened up process for fast-tracking patent approval for green energy projects. http://bit.ly/j0KV2U

126. Eliminated Bush-era restrictions on embryonic stem cell research, and provided increased federal support for biomedical and stem cell research. http://bit.ly/h36SSO   http://ti.me/edezge

127. Through the American Recovery and Reinvestment Act, committed more federal funding, about $18 billion, to support non-defense science and research labs. http://nyti.ms/fTs9t7

128. Signed Democratic-sponsored Christopher and Dana Reeve Paralysis Act, the first comprehensive attempt to improve the lives of Americans living with paralysis. http://bit.ly/fOi2rb

129. Expanded the Nurse-Family Partnership program, which provides home visits by trained registered nurses to low-income expectant mothers and their families, to cover more first-time mothers. http://bit.ly/jRRRJc

130. Obama EPA reversed research ethics standards which allowed humans to be used as "guinea pigs" in tests of the effects of chemicals, to comply with numerous codes of medical ethics. http://bit.ly/bKgqdS

131. Conducted a cyberspace policy review. http://1.usa.gov/gmbdvC

132. Provided financial support for private sector space programs. http://bit.ly/fn8ucr

133. Oversaw enhanced earth mapping, to provide valuable data for agricultural, educational, scientific, and government use. http://bit.ly/dNTRyP

134. Along with Democrats in Congress, ushered through and signed a bill authorizing FDA to regulate tobacco. http://on.msnbc.com/fiKViB as a result, the FDA has Ordered Tobacco Companies to Disclose Cigarette Ingredients and banned sale of cigarettes falsely labeled as "light."

135. Through American Recovery and Reinvestment Act, provided $500 million for Health Professions Training Programs. http://bit.ly/ecQSgA

136. Increased funding for community-based prevention programs. http://bit.ly/frMPG3

137. Oversaw a 50% decrease in cost of prescription drugs for seniors. http://bit.ly/e5b1iq   http://1.usa.gov/fVNkt9

138. Eliminated the Bush-era practice of forbidding Medicare from negotiating with drug companies on price. http://bit.ly/fOkG5b

139. Two weeks after taking office, signed Democratic-sponsored Children's Health Insurance Reauthorization Act, which increased the number of children covered by health insurance by 4 million. http://bit.ly/fDEzGv

140. Urged Congress to investigate Anthem Blue Cross for raising premiums 39% without explanation. Democratic Rep. Waxman responded by launching a probe, and Anthem Blue Cross put increase on hold for two months. http://yhoo.it/e8Tj9C

141. Ushered through and signed Affordable Care Act, which expanded health insurance coverage to at least 30 million more people, ended many common insurance company practices that are often detrimental to those with coverage. He also established healthcare.gov, so that taxpayers could keep up with developments. http://www.healthcare.gov/

142. Through ACA, allowed children to be covered under their parents' policy until they turned 26. http://nyti.ms/fNB26V

143. Through the ACA, provided tax breaks to allow 3.5 million small business to provide health insurance to their employees, and 29 million people will receive tax breaks to help them afford health insurance. http://nyti.ms/fNB26V

144. Through the ACA, expanded Medicaid to those making up to 133% of the federal poverty level. http://nyti.ms/ekMWpo

145. Through the ACA, health insurance companies now have to disclose how much of your premium actually goes to pay for patient care. http://nyti.ms/fNB26V

146. Provisions in the ACA have already resulted in Medicare costs actually declining slightly this fiscal year, for the first time in many years, according to the Congressional Budget Office. The increase in 2011 was 4%, which is very low compared to the average 12% annual inflation rate during previous 40 years. http://1.usa.gov/oMxpTh

He Took Steps to Strengthen the Middle Class and Families, and to Fight Poverty

147. Worked to provide affordable, high-quality child care to working families. http://bit.ly/fNfidS

148. Cracked down on companies that were previously denying sick pay, vacation and health insurance, and Social Security and Medicare tax payments through abuse of the employee classification of independent contractor. http://nyti.ms/fOGLcj

149. Through the American Recovery and Reinvestment Act , cut taxes for 95% of America's working families.   http://bit.ly/eSEI4F

150. Tax rates for average working families are the lowest since 1950. http://bit.ly/f74pD8

151. Extended and fully funded the patch for the Alternative Minimum Tax for 10 years. http://bit.ly/eFeSdP

152. Extended discounted COBRA health coverage for the unemployed from 9 months to 15 months, and he's extended unemployment benefits several times. http://aol.it/evtVxD   http://nyti.ms/emrqKJ   http://bit.ly/hOtlpg http://bit.ly/fTT7kz

153. Provided a $20 billion increase for the Supplemental Nutrition Assistance Program (Food Stamps). http://nyti.ms/gfLqyM

154. Signed an Executive Order that established the White House Office of Urban Affairs. http://wapo.st/eWECA8

He Took Concrete Steps to Improve Our Environment and Address Our Energy Needs

155. Fast-tracked regulations to allow states to enact fuel efficiency standards that exceeded federal standards.   http://nyti.ms/e8e94x

156. Fast-tracked increased fuel economy standards for vehicles beginning with the 2011 model year. It was the first time such standards had been increased in a decade.   http://politi.co/hiaPKM

157. Oversaw establishment of an Energy Partnership for the Americas, to create more markets for American-made biofuels and green energy technologies. http://bit.ly/lZp73y

158. Obama EPA reversed a Bush-era decision to allow the largest mountaintop removal project in US history.   http://bit.ly/lP3yEL

159. Ordered the Department of Energy to implement more aggressive efficiency standards for common household appliances.   http://1.usa.gov/g3MTbu

160. Ordered energy plants to prepare to produce at least 15% of all energy through renewable resources like wind and solar, by 2021. http://reut.rs/fV155p (As you can see, Republicans are trying hard to kill it.)

161. Oversaw the creation of an initiative that converts old factories and manufacturing centers into new clean technology centers. http://bit.ly/mjnq2R

162. Bypassed Republican opposition in Congress and ordered EPA to begin regulating and measuring carbon emissions. http://bit.ly/froaP5

163. Obama EPA ruled that CO2 is a pollutant. http://bit.ly/iQTSNN

164. Oversaw doubling federal spending on clean energy research. http://bit.ly/iN0sCE

165. Pushed through a tax credit to help people buy plug-in hybrid cars. http://bit.ly/j8UP5Y

166. Created a program to develop renewable energy projects on the waters of our Outer Continental Shelf that will produce electricity from wind, wave, and ocean currents. http://1.usa.gov/fgfRWq

167. Reengaged in the climate change and greenhouse gas emissions agreements talks, and proposed one himself. He also addressed the U.N. Climate Change Conference, officially reversing the Bush era stance that climate change was a "hoax." http://bit.ly/dX6Vj3 http://bit.ly/fE2PxK http://nyti.ms/hfeqvv

168. Fully supported the initial phase of the creation of a legally-binding treaty to reduce mercury emissions worldwide. http://bit.ly/eJ6QOO

169. Required states to provide incentives to utilities to reduce their energy consumption. http://bit.ly/lBhk7P

170. Following the neglect of Bush's eight year reign, he reengaged in a number of treaties and agreements designed to protect the Antarctic. http://bit.ly/fzQUFO

171. Created tax write-offs for purchases of hybrid automobiles, and later he and Democrats morphed that program into one that includes electric cars. http://bit.ly/glCukV

172. Mandated that federal government fleet purchases be for fuel-efficient American vehicles, and encouraged that federal agencies support experimental, fuel-efficient vehicles. http://bit.ly/h5KZqy http://1.usa.gov/fLWq5c http://1.usa.gov/hmUSbk

173. Oversaw and pushed through amendment to the Oil Pollution Act of 1990 authorizing advances from Oil Spill Liability Trust Fund for the Deepwater Horizon oil spill. http://1.usa.gov/yTRYVo

174. Actively tried to amend the Oil Pollution Act of 1990 to eliminate the liability limits for those companies responsible for large oil spills. http://nyti.ms/bxjDi3

175. Initiated Criminal and Civil inquiries into the Deepwater Horizon oil spill. http://nyti.ms/bVuB7a

176. Through his EPA, he asserted federal legal supremacy, and barred Texas from authorizing new refinery permits on its own. http://bit.ly/ww8eMd

177. Strengthened the Endangered Species Act. http://bit.ly/hscjsH

178. Obama EPA improved boiler safety standards to improve air quality, and save 6500 lives per year. http://bit.ly/jYH7nt

179. Through the EPA, attempted to take steps to severely limit the use of antibiotics in livestock feed, to increase their efficacy in humans. http://bit.ly/fBuWd2

180. Increased funding for National Parks and Forests by 10% http://bit.ly/fbJPjY

181. Announced greatly improved commercial fuel efficiency standards. http://1.usa.gov/oQiC1K

182. Announced a huge increase in average fuel economy standards from 27.5mpg in 2010 to 35.5mpg starting in 2016 and 54.5 starting in 2025 http://1.usa.gov/qtghsW

But that's not All...

183. Expanded trade agreements to include stricter labor and environmental agreements such as NAFTA. http://bit.ly/etznpY

184. Oversaw funding of the design of a new Smithsonian National Museum of African American History, which is scheduled to open on the National Mall in 2015. He protected the funding during the recent budget negotiations. http://on.fb.me/fD0EVO   http://bit.ly/ff5Luv

185. Oversaw and passed increased funding for the National Endowment for the Arts. http://bit.ly/dFb8qF

186. Nominated Sonia Sotomayor and Elena Kagan to the Supreme Court. Sotomayor is the first Hispanic Justice in the court's history, and the women represent only the third and fourth women to serve on the court, out of a total of 112 justices. http://huff.to/eOChg6 http://bit.ly/i02wgP

187. Appointed the most diverse Cabinet in history, including more women than any other incoming president. http://bit.ly/dX6vNB

188. Eliminated federal funding for abstinence-only education, and rescinded the global gag rule. http://bit.ly/eCFAI1 http://bit.ly/f92drF

189. Loosened the rules and allowed the 14 states that legalized medical marijuana to regulate themselves without federal interference. http://huff.to/eQfa7j

190. Signed national service legislation, increasing funding for national service groups, including triple the size of the Americorps program. http://bit.ly/idgQH5

191. Signed an Executive Order that will speed up deployment of a more comprehensive broadband infrastructure. http://1.usa.gov/M7rVpe

192. Signed an Executive Order creating jobs immediately by instructing them to reduce the time needed for review and permitting of infrastructure projects. http://1.usa.gov/GHxaYt

193. Signed a bill that provided $4.3 billion in additional assistance to 9/11 first responders. http://bit.ly/o7cWYS

And Did You Know?

194. Despite the characterizations of some, Obama's success rate in winning congressional votes on issues was an unprecedented 96.7% for his first year in office. Though he is often cited as superior to Obama, President Lyndon Johnson's success rate in 1965 was only 93%. http://n.pr/i3d7cY

Thank You **"The PCTC Blog"** for this wonderful list and the citations that went with them.

Now that is one great list that will go down in history as one of the greatest first terms ever.

OK people let's not keep this a secret from you friends.

OBAMACARE: Patient Protection and Affordable Care Act

We have heard nothing buy lies from the Republicans about Obamacare and here is a great list of what is covers.

Thank you www.reddit.com for the summary:

Okay, explained like you're a five year-old (well, okay, maybe a bit older), without too much oversimplification, and (hopefully) without sounding too biased:

What people call "Obamacare" is actually the Patient Protection and Affordable Care Act. However, people were calling it "Obamacare" before everyone even hammered out what it would be. It's a term mostly used by people who don't like the PPACA, and it's become popularized in part because PPACA is a really long and awkward name, even when you turn it into an acronym like that.

Anyway, the PPACA made a bunch of new rules regarding health care, with the purpose of making health care more affordable for everyone. Opponents of the PPACA, on the other hand, feel that the rules it makes take away too many freedoms and force people (both individuals and businesses) to do things they shouldn't have to.

So what does it do? Well, here is everything, in the order of when it goes into effect (because some of it happens later than other parts of it):

Already in effect:
It allows the Food and Drug Administration to approve more generic drugs (making for more competition in the market to drive down prices)
It increases the rebates on drugs people get through Medicare (so drugs cost less)
It establishes a non-profit group, that the government doesn't directly control, PCORI, to study different kinds of treatments to see what works better and is the best use of money. (Citation: Page 665, sec. 1181)
It makes chain restaurants like McDonalds display how many calories are in all of their foods, so people can have an easier time making choices to eat healthy. (Citation: Page 499, sec. 4205)

It makes a "high-risk pool" for people with pre-existing conditions. Basically, this is a way to slowly ease into getting rid of "pre-existing conditions" altogether. For now, people who already have health issues that would be considered "pre-existing conditions" can still get insurance, but at different rates than people without them.

It renews some old policies, and calls for the appointment of various positions.

It creates a new 10% tax on indoor tanning booths. (Citation: Page 923, sec. 5000B)

It says that health insurance companies can no longer tell customers that they won't get any more coverage because they have hit a "lifetime limit". Basically, if someone has paid for health insurance, that company can't tell that person that he's used that insurance too much throughout his life so they won't cover him any more. They can't do this for lifetime spending, and they're limited in how much they can do this for yearly spending. (Citation: Page 14, sec. 2711)

Kids can continue to be covered by their parents' health insurance until they're 26.

No more "pre-existing conditions" for kids under the age of 19.

Insurers have less ability to change the amount customers have to pay for their plans.

People in a "Medicare Gap" get a rebate to make up for the extra money they would otherwise have to spend.

Insurers can't just drop customers once they get sick. (Citation: Page 14, sec. 2712)

Insurers have to tell customers what they're spending money on. (Instead of just "administrative fee", they have to be more specific).

Insurers need to have an appeals process for when they turn down a claim, so customers have some manner of recourse other than a lawsuit when they're turned down.

New ways to stop fraud are created.

Medicare extends to smaller hospitals.

Medicare patients with chronic illnesses must be monitored more thoroughly.

Reduces the costs for some companies that handle benefits for the elderly.

A new website is made to give people insurance and health information. (I think this is it: http://www.healthcare.gov/).

A credit program is made that will make it easier for business to invest in new ways to treat illness.

A limit is placed on just how much of a percentage of the money an insurer makes can be profit, to make sure they're not price-gouging customers.

A limit is placed on what type of insurance accounts can be used to pay for over-the-counter drugs without a prescription. Basically, your insurer isn't paying for the Aspirin you bought for that hangover.

Employers need to list the benefits they provided to employees on their tax forms.

8/1/2012
Any health plans sold after this date must provide preventative care (mammograms, colonoscopies, etc.) without requiring any sort of co-pay or charge.

1/1/2013
If you make over $200,000 a year, your taxes go up a tiny bit (0.9%). Edit: To address those who take issue with the word "tiny", a change of 0.9% is relatively tiny. Any look at how taxes have fluctuated over the years will reveal that a change of less than one percent is miniscule, especially when we're talking about people in the top 5% of earners.

1/1/2014
This is when a lot of the really big changes happen.
No more "pre-existing conditions". At all. People will be charged the same regardless of their medical history.
If you can afford insurance but do not get it, you will be charged a fee. This is the "mandate" that people are talking about. Basically, it's a trade-off for the "pre-existing conditions" bit, saying that since insurers now have to cover you regardless of what you have, you can't just wait to buy insurance until you get sick. Otherwise no one would buy insurance until they needed it. You can opt not to get insurance, but you'll have to pay the fee instead, unless of course you're not buying insurance because you just can't afford it.
Insurers now can't do annual spending caps. Their customers can get as much health care in a given year as they need. (Citation: Page 14, sec. 2711)
Make it so more poor people can get Medicaid by making the low-income cut-off higher.
Small businesses get some tax credits for two years.
Businesses with over 50 employees must offer health insurance to full-time employees, or pay a penalty.
Limits how high of an annual deductible insurers can charge customers.
Cut some Medicare spending
Place a $2500 limit on tax-free spending on FSAs (accounts for medical spending). Basically, people using these accounts now have to pay taxes on any money over $2500 they put into them.
Establish health insurance exchanges and rebates for the lower and middle-class, basically making it so they have an easier time getting affordable medical coverage.
Congress and Congressional staff will only be offered the same insurance offered to people in the insurance exchanges, rather than Federal Insurance. Basically,

we won't be footing their health care bills any more than any other American citizen.
A new tax on pharmaceutical companies.
A new tax on the purchase of medical devices.
A new tax on insurance companies based on their market share. Basically, the more of the market they control, the more they'll get taxed.
The amount you can deduct from your taxes for medical expenses increases.

1/1/2015
Doctors' pay will be determined by the quality of their care, not how many people they treat. Edit: a_real_MD addresses questions regarding this one in far more detail and with far more expertise than I can offer in this post. If you're looking for a more in-depth explanation of this one (as many of you are), I highly recommend you give his post a read.

1/1/2017
If any state can come up with their own plan, one which gives citizens the same level of care at the same price as the PPACA, they can ask the Secretary of Health and Human Resources for permission to do their plan instead of the PPACA. So if they can get the same results without, say, the mandate, they can be allowed to do so. Vermont, for example, has expressed a desire to just go straight to single-payer (in simple terms, everyone is covered, and medical expenses are paid by taxpayers).

2018
All health care plans must now cover preventative care (not just the new ones).
A new tax on "Cadillac" health care plans (more expensive plans for rich people who want fancier coverage).

2020
The elimination of the "Medicare gap"

— original source, with hyperlinks to citations:
http://www.reddit.com/tb/vbkfm

Now lets take a minute and look at Mitt Romney and President Barrack Obama and when they speak to the people. Romney seems fake because he has no compassion for the people he seeks only the power of the office.

When the President speaks you can feel the compassion he feels for the people. I wrote this quote and I see the President right up there with the Kennedy's and Martin Luther King.
Men, who felt the pulse of the American people and tried their best to represent them.

"When we talk about inspiration and who can give us that inspiration in the political world I see a common denominator in those who inspire, they speak from the heart with passion and foremost they speak about the people and for the people!"
Jeff Carlson

REVIEW THE ISSUES FACING THE COUNTRY

The Supreme Court

Is in my opinion the number one issue for the 2012 election because as many as three new judges will be appointed.

This country cannot allow the Party of Scrooge to add to the list of Idiots that gave us Citizen United and in 2000 appointed BUSH as the President even though we now know that Gore had won the Election if allowed to be re-counted.

On the ruling on Citizen United two quotes:

"One of the stupidest rulings ever consummated or perpetrated on the American people."
Jimmy Carter

"A major victory for big oil, Wall Street banks, health insurance companies and the other powerful interests that marshal their power every day in Washington to drown out the voices of everyday Americans."
President Barack Obama was a major critic

Now that Romney is going to lead the GOP we must look at the people he is surrounding himself with, and Robert Bork, is as good as any reason to make sure Romney never gets to Smell the White House Steps.

Romney to "BORK" the Country

"Robert Bork is a right-wing ideologue. As a Supreme Court Justice, he would show little respect for the past 30 years of judicial precedent. Acting on dogmatic, narrow-minded views, he might vote to overrule landmark decisions on abortion, civil rights and church-state separation."
Time Magazine --- Before he was turned down as a Supreme Court Justice

In March 2002, the Oxford English Dictionary added an entry for the verb "Bork" as U.S. political slang, with this definition:
"To defame or vilify (a person) systematically, esp. in the mass media, usually with the aim of preventing his or her appointment to public office; to obstruct or thwart (a person) in this way."

Robert Bork was turned down as a Supreme Court Justice!!!!!

Note from Me:
SEEMS that BUSH slipped in more than one BORK onto the Current Supreme Court.

BORK wants to set this country back so far there was no constitution or country. Robert Bork :
1. Is opposed to Civil Rights.
2. Has indicated that there is no right to contraception, even within the confines of marriage.
3. Opposed to the recognition of the Right of Free Speech for anything except political philosophy, and has specifically opposed the notion that science is protected by the First Amendment.
4. Supportive of laws that attempt to control the identity of people with whom anyone can have sex.
5. Committed to the notion that the Constitution does NOT shield women from gender discrimination.

Four of the current Supreme Court Justices are over age 70. One of these justices is a cancer survivor. So whoever takes the oath of office in 2013 will likely have the opportunity to fill several of these seats. Now that Romney has selected Bork as one of his chief judicial advisers, all Americans should be focused on the fact that Robert Bork could determine the identity of the next several Supreme Court Justices.

Robert Bork could determine the identity of several of the next Supreme Court Justices.

Medicare

Republicans want to end it and give us a Voucher System

"Do you know what the overhead is of the Medicare system? One-point-zero-five percent. Do you know what - private insurance is 30 percent in overhead and profits? Given a choice how I'm going to improve health care, I'm going to take it away from private insurance profits and overhead. Wouldn't you?"
Anthony Weiner

Medicare --- we have seen in the RYAN bill they want to end Medicare as we know it and create a voucher system that will not cover anything for most seniors. Suicide would be rampant amongst seniors. Things to think about this is a payroll deduction and we all have been paying on this INSURANCE since we started working --- WHO IS getting our money under Ryan's Bill -- he wants to give another 37% tax break for the upper 1% that's who.

Medicaid ---Something for all us to think about is in the Ryan Bill they will remove one third of the payments to Medicaid. Now what most people do not realize is that is the money used to support Nursing Homes and the poorest of the poor..

Under the Ryan bill they are estimating that half the Nursing Homes would be closed, now it means millions of people losing their jobs but even worse, where are those Nursing Home residents going to go? Will they be left to the families to support and take care of them?
Are you prepared to take care of you elderly parents? Under the Ryan bill you will be making that decision to step up or let them die in the street.

Everyone knows people that have had to go to Nursing Homes, if it is someone in your family are you prepared to take care of these people? If not, you need to vote for the Democrats.

Five things to know about Medicare:
1 There are 47.5 million people receiving Medicare in the US

2. Before Medicare over half the seniors had no health care coverage

3. Seniors can get free preventative screenings, like Mammograms. Diabetes and Cancer Screenings thanks to Health Care Reform called Obamacare.

4. Medicare is more cost efficient than private firms showing a lower cost growth for the last 30 years

5. New crack downs on fraud and abuse returned a record 5.4 billion dollars to Medicare for years 2010 and 2011

Note Medicare needs some work --- Number one is to be able to negotiate with DRUG companies on the Price of Drugs would slash 30 to 50% of the current cost of Medicare Part D.

Social Security

Republicans want to privatize and hand the surplus to Wall Street is the bottom line. It will be a battle we will need to fight over and over.

Social Security ---- They want to privatize it and that means the 2.7 trillion surplus will be handed over to Wall Street and Fees will be attached meaning at least 10 % will be going to pay bonuses to the people who destroyed the economy.

All Presidents since Reagan started it have borrowed against the Funds meaning those funds are on paper only, WALL STREET has told the Party of Scrooge they want that money so look out.

In the 2012 election we have choices and none more straight forward than Social Security.

The Democrats want to preserve and protect and improve Social Security.

The Party of Scrooge wants to hand the money to Wall Street and privatize it.

If you are a Senior you must vote Democrat or watch your money be handed to the people that just destroyed the economy then got bailed out and then paid themselves huge bonuses.

YOUR CHOICE --- Seems rather simple to me

"Privatizing Social Security doesn't make sense, and it's out of step with the fundamental value of ensuring that after a life spent working hard and contributing to the greatness of our nation, every American should have a secure retirement."
Debbie Stabenow, United States Senator from Michigan.

"Should any political party attempt to abolish social security, unemployment insurance, and eliminate labor laws and farm programs, you would not hear of that party again in our political history. There is a tiny splinter group, of course, that believes that you can do these things. Among them are a few Texas oil millionaires, and an occasional politician or businessman from other areas. Their number is negligible and they are stupid."
Dwight D. Eisenhower The Last great Republican

This would be the plan they would use:

First thing is they would cut off all those under the age of 55 and tell them all the money they have been paying into Social Security since the day they started working has now been given to Wall Street. They will be left on their own to try and save for their retirement, good luck on that.

Second thing they will do for those over 55 they will give them some options. One will be to collect a grand sum once they retire, the second will be to figure out how many years you will receive Social Security. Here is what do not understand you will no longer be covered until you die.

Here is the catch no new money will be going into the funds and like Bill Clinton declared do the Arithmetic, those funds will be depleted fast by Wall Street in fees and Bonus and all the Funds will be gone and so will any payments to those still remaining.

This is a sure Death Penalty to most seniors.

Education a full out attack to end public education

Education ---- you can look at how they are attacking teachers at a state and somewhat national level. This is about busting the teachers unions and getting the system set for Vouchers and Private Schools with Public Education ended or just not funded.

WHY America according to the Chamber of Commerce we no longer need a Middle Class or people with education --- But they must continue to educate the RICH and they want to POOR to pay for them.

"To the extent that we are all educated and informed, we will be more equipped to deal with the gut issues that tend to divide us."
Caroline Kennedy Schlossberg Daughter of the late President John Kennedy

Education what scares the GOP more than anything is a Education system that is fair to all.

Never has Education been under attack as it is right now as the Republicans are fighting for a Race to the Bottom.

They have attacked the Teachers all over the country and want to destroy the unions that protect them.

They want to privatize the entire school system so that they can control the school curriculum.

Again this is a CHOICE we have and will be a challenge moving forward in the coming years

"We have to be careful not to succumb to this nonsense that a public system is inherently flawed and that therefore we have to turn to the marketplace for solutions. I've never in my entire life seen any evidence that the competitive free market, unrestricted, without a strong counterpoise within the public sector, will ever dispense decent medical care, sanitation, transportation, or education to the people. It's as simple as that."
--Jonathan Kozol, author of "Savage Inequalities" and "Amazing Grace."

"The real equity issue is that there are radically unequal allocations of funds to schools. These unequal allocations routinely disadvantage schools in central cities and in poor rural areas. Private school choice, as it is currently being proposed, is a smokescreen to avoid tackling this real equity issue."
--Linda Darling-Hammond, professor of teaching and teacher education at Stanford University.

"Voucher proposals take many forms, and some are designed to deliberately disguise the basic realities that will result over time. The best students will be skimmed off -- those whom private schools find desirable for their own reasons. Since families will have to make up additional costs, those in the upper-and middle-income brackets will be helped the most -- as long as their kids don't have personal, behavioral, or educational challenges that cause the private school to pass them by."
-- Kweisi Mfume, president and CEO of the NAACP

"The conservatives made me their poster girl as long as it appeared I was supporting their case. And now I am the odd person out. They want the religious schools to be tax-supported. Blacks and poor are being used to help legitimize them as the power group."
-- Rep. Annette (Polly) Williams, the African-American legislator from Milwaukee who for many years was the leading spokesperson for vouchers. Williams made the statement to USA Today in the spring of 1999.

You will hear much about how we should destroy the Public Education System and go to a Voucher System.

This would be a disaster that this country might not recover from and here is why:

1. By doing this the public will now be paying for the wealthy kids to go to Private Schools.

2. By allowing this you would see the Private Schools Cherry Pick the Students they want to attend their schools.

3. Control the Curriculum. We have seen in TEXAS and a few other states where the History Books are full of LIES. Joe McCarthy saved us from the COMMIES. We Won the Vietnam War. There were mass amounts of WMD found in IRAQ and BUSH saved America by attacking them.

4. Teachers and unions would take a huge hit. Religion and Right Wing Ideology would be rammed down the throats of our kids using every brainwashing method known to man to stop free thinkers.

Here is a Quote from a Article talking about what Walker is doing to Wisconsin and it is not good.

Mike Langyel, the head of the Milwaukee Teachers' Education Association, was emotional in a phone call to discuss the budget proposal, which he called **"a direct attack on public education in Milwaukee."**

"In a time of budget cuts, the governor is going to subsidize the tuition of wealthy families by removing the income caps, so that will be an added burden to state government"

CRITICAL THINKING

Why does the Republican Party fear critical thinking?

For those who do not know the Republicans want to eliminate Critical Thinking from all levels of education.

"When a Political Party makes it a policy to eliminate Critical Thinking, this Party must fear that knowledge and analysis of their Party would lead to people leaving the Party"
Jeff Carlson

Why Critical Thinking?
Everyone thinks; it is our nature to do so. But much of our thinking, left to itself, is biased, distorted, partial, uninformed or down-right prejudiced. Yet the quality of our life and that of what we produce, make, or build depends precisely on the quality of our thought. Shoddy thinking is costly, both in money and in quality of life. Excellence in thought, however, must be systematically cultivated.

A Definition
Critical thinking is that mode of thinking - about any subject, content, or problem - in which the thinker improves the quality of his or her thinking by skillfully taking charge of the structures inherent in thinking and imposing intellectual standards upon them.

Brief Conceptualization of Critical Thinking:

"Critical thinking is self-guided, self-disciplined thinking which attempts to reason at the highest level of quality in a fair-minded way. People who think critically consistently attempt to live rationally, reasonably, empathically. They are keenly aware of the inherently flawed nature of human thinking when left unchecked. They strive to diminish the power of their egocentric and sociocentric tendencies.

They use the intellectual tools that critical thinking offers – concepts and principles that enable them to analyze, assess, and improve thinking. They work diligently to develop the intellectual virtues of intellectual integrity, intellectual humility, intellectual civility, intellectual empathy, intellectual sense of justice and confidence in reason.

They realize that no matter how skilled they are as thinkers, they can always improve their reasoning abilities and they will at times fall prey to mistakes in reasoning, human irrationality, prejudices, biases, distortions, uncritically accepted social rules and taboos, self-interest, and vested interest.

They strive to improve the world in whatever ways they can and contribute to a more rational, civilized society. At the same time, they recognize the complexities often inherent in doing so.

They avoid thinking simplistically about complicated issues and strive to appropriately consider the rights and needs of relevant others. They recognize the complexities in developing as thinkers, and commit themselves to life-long practice toward self-improvement.

They embody the Socratic principle: The unexamined life is not worth living, because they realize that many unexamined lives together result in an uncritical, unjust, dangerous world."

~ Linda Elder, September, 2007

Famous Quotes about Critical Thinking:

Each of the following quotes either exemplifies critical thought, or illuminates a problem in human thought which critical thinking addresses.

"You assist an evil system most effectively by obeying its orders and decrees. An evil system never deserves such allegiance. Allegiance to it means partaking of the evil. A good person will resist an evil system with his or her whole soul."
~ Mahatma Gandhi

"During times of universal deceit, telling the truth becomes a revolutionary act."
~ George Orwell

"The trouble with the world is that the stupid are cocksure and the intelligent are full of doubt."
~ Bertrand Russell

"The shepherd always tries to persuade the sheep that their interests and his own are the same."
~ Stendhal

"The great masses of the people...will more easily fall victims to a big lie than to a small one."
~ Adolf Hitler, Mein Kampf, 1933

"The will of the people is the only legitimate foundation of any government, and to protect its free expression should be our first object."
~ Thomas Jefferson, First Inaugural Address, 1801

We cannot allow the Republicans to destroy our education system, just another great reason to vote straight Democrat until we see a human side to the Republican Party.

EPA a full out attack on the environment

EPA --- and other departments that oversee Corporations are under attack ---the Party of Scrooge wants zero regulations and proudly admits that they can regulate themselves.

Can you imagine the Koch Brothers doing anything but polluting.

Clean AIR, Fresh Water, Food supplies that we can eat that will not kill us, toys that will not harm our kids, drugs that will not kill you --- these are all at stake.

We must all know that many changes have to be made to the EPA in order to restore it back to what it once was before the Bush Administration dismantled it and stacked the agency with Corporate insiders.

In 2012 we have choices and again we have the GOP attacking the EPA and the Democrats trying hard to keep the EPA in place and make it stronger.

Here was a headline from Huffington Post as the House ends its session and was heading home for the Election:

"House Passes Sweeping Anti-Environmental Bill as Final Business before Elections"

This bill attacks the EPA and every regulation that keeps the Air and Water safe from the likes of the Koch Brothers.

After reviewing the Bill the EPA released this statement:

"The Environmental Protection Agency estimates that emissions reductions resulting from meeting these standards will prevent as many as 11,000 avoidable premature deaths and 4,700 heart attacks annually," reads a Statement of Administration Policy, issued Thursday by the Office of Management and Budget.

Every single Republican voted for the bill and you can add in 17 Blue Dog Democrats that betrayed the American People.

The Koch Brothers the worse polluter in the country are behind almost all the attacks and they control the Tea Party.

What kind of a world do we want to leave our Grand Kids?

That is why in 2012 you only have one choice to save the environment for the next generation

"What kind of world do we want for our Kids our Grand Kids, all creatures want to protect their own, we must do every thing in our power, to save our water, to save our environment, from the most destructive source on earth, Man"
Jeff Carlson

Republican congressmen take aim at Environmental Protection Agency

"Since assuming control of the U.S. House of Representatives
in January, Republicans have passed at least 300 bills, riders
and amendments designed to scale back environmental regulations they say stymie job creation. Opposition by most Senate Democrats and the Obama administration have stopped the measures from becoming law, but that could change if the GOP holds onto the House, unseats enough Democrats to win a majority in the Senate and wins the White House in next year's elections."
By: Jeff Carlson

Rep. Cedric Richmond, D-New Orleans, said EPA
has a **"legal responsibility and moral duty to respond"**
when it finds environmental hazards.

"There is a place for responsible environmental regulations,
especially when we're talking about keeping our families and
our children safe," Richmond said. "Regulations aren't standing
in the way of job creation. The U.S. Chamber of Commerce's own poll showed that uncertainty about the economy -- not regulations -- is why small businesses aren't hiring."

Rep. Henry Waxman, D-Calif., goes even further in his criticism.
"This is the most anti-environmental House of Representatives in history," .

REPUBLICAN HOUSE MEMBERS ON ENVIRONMENT

This is just since 2011

Another reason to vote every single one out of office

House Republicans Voted against the Environment More Than 300 Times Since 2011
– --133 votes targeting the Environmental Protection Agency
– – 54 target the Department of Energy
– – 128 block measures preventing pollution
– – 55 to de-fund or repeal clean energy initiatives
– – 47 votes to promote offshore drilling

"You must teach your children that the ground beneath their feet is the ashes of your grandfathers. So that they will respect the land, tell your children that the earth is rich with the lives of our kin. Teach your children what we have taught our children, that the earth is our mother. Whatever befalls the earth befalls the sons of the earth. If men spit upon the ground, they spit upon themselves."
Chief Seattle Born 1780's died 1866 led the Duwamish and Suquamish Tribes

"I think the environment should be put in the category of our national security. Defense of our resources is just as important as defense abroad. Otherwise what is there to defend?"
Robert Redford

FDA

While the Koch Brothers fund attacks on the EPA, Monsanto is attacking the FDA and they want every single regulation removed and they do not want any investigation into how they conduct their Business.

"The nation that destroys its soil, destroys itself."
--- Franklin Delano Roosevelt

"Essentially, all life depends upon the soil ... There can be no life without soil and no soil without life; they have evolved together."
~ Charles E. Kellogg, USDA Yearbook of Agriculture, 1939

"...the Latin name for man, homo, derived from humus, the stuff of life in the soil."
~ Dr. Daniel Hillel Professor of Soil Physics and Hydrology, University of Massachusetts

"We know more about the movement of celestial bodies than about the soil underfoot."
~ Leonardo DaVinci, circa 1500s

"Probably more harm has been done to the science by the almost universal attempts to look upon the soil merely as a producer of crops than as a natural body worth in and for itself of all the study that can be devoted to it, than most men realize."
~ C.F. Marbut, 1920 was soil scientist, professor of geology

Wikipedia on Monsanto:

The Monsanto Company (NYSE: MON) is a multinational agricultural biotechnology corporation. It is the world's leading producer of the herbicide glyphosate, marketed in the Roundup brand, and in other brands. Monsanto is also the second largest producer of genetically engineered (GE) seed; it provides the technology in 49% of the genetically engineered seeds used in the US market. It is headquartered in Creve Coeur, Missouri.

Agracetus, owned by Monsanto, exclusively produces Roundup Ready soybean seed for the commercial market. In 2005, it finalized the purchase of Seminis Inc, making it the world's largest conventional seed company a the time. In 2012, its competitors sold more GE corn and soybean seed than Monsanto due to price resistance from farmers.

Monsanto's development and marketing of genetically engineered seed and bovine growth hormone, as well as its aggressive litigation, political lobbying practices, seed commercialization practices and "strong-arming" of the seed industry have made the company controversial around the world and a primary target of the alter-globalization movement and environmental activists.

In 2009 Monsanto came under scrutiny from the U.S. Justice Department, which began investigating whether the company's activities in the soybean markets were breaking anti-trust rules

Monsanto is notable for its involvement in high profile lawsuits, as both plaintiff and defendant. It has been involved in a number of class action suits, where fines and damages have run into the hundreds of millions of dollars, usually over health issues related to its products. Monsanto has also made frequent use of the courts to defend its patents, particularly in the area of biotechnology.

After reading many Articles about them, I feel there is so much more that needs to be looked into.

I can say this about them, they are the company behind the GOP to end the FDA and they are way to big and need to be broken up.

I did a Quote of the Day about what's killing the bees and it all points back to Monsanto. Of course they are so big and powerful we will never get the answers unless we the people demand it.

I pointed out that we are getting fatter and Autism is on the rise and I am sure these are all connected but again that is my mine connecting the Dots and the Facts have not been proven.

Excerpt from article about Monsanto:
Monsantos' Roundup (Glyphosate): The Science Vs. Marketing

2011 was a watershed year, as far as scientific revelations into the nature and extent of the damage associated with glyphosate-based herbicide usage and exposure is concerned.

An accumulating body of peer-reviewed and published research now indicates glyphosate may be contributing to several dozen adverse health effects in exposed populations.

And as we shall see, human exposure is as universal as is the contamination of our food, air, rain and groundwater with this now ubiquitous chemical .

Ever since Monsanto developed, marketed and patented the glyphosate molecule -- Roundup (-) herbicide's active ingredient -- beginning in the early 70's, a substantial and ever-growing portion of the earth's arable surface has been transformed into an environmental and human health experiment, of unprecedented scale.

WHAT IS KILLING THE BEES?

Funny how my mine works but as I listen to the news and I hear bees dying, the population getting fatter, and autism on the rise and I see a connection, that connection is the food supply and Monsanto.

We know that the Koch Brothers has paid off the Party of Scrooge / GOP to end the EPA. Now lets look at who is pushing Scrooge to end the FDA not to hard to figure it out --- MONSANTO who else.

Monsanto already has major controls over the FDA so this should be high on our list of Progressive things to do after we do a clean sweep of the GOP / Tea Party / Party of Scrooge.

Get the FDA to find out just what kind of monster that Monsanto has created and can we reverse it so our kids and grand kids can survive.

"So goes the Honey Bee so goes the Human Race."
Jeff Carlson

Article "What is killing the Bees" Overview:

Pneumatic drilling machines suck the seeds in and spray them with the insecticide to create a coating before they are planted in the ground. Researchers suspected the mass die-offs could have been caused by the particles of insecticide that were released into the air by the machines when the chemicals are sprayed.

Honeybees are critical for pollinating food crops. Scientists
say the disruption of pollination could dramatically affect
entire ecosystems. In addition, as the researchers wrote in the study,

"In view of the currently increasing crop production, and also of corn as a renewable energy source, the correct use of these insecticides within sustainable agriculture is a cause of concern."

Quotes from Professor Dee Carter, from the University of Sydney's School of Molecular and Microbial Biosciences.

"The honey is distinctive in that it comes only from bees feeding off tea trees native to Australia and New Zealand".

"Honey sounds very homey and unscientific, which is why we needed the science to validate the claims made for it,"

"The curative properties of various types of honey have been known to indigenous cultures for thousands of years, and dressing wounds with honey was common before the advent of antibiotics."

"Most bacteria that cause infections in hospitals are resistant to at least one antibiotic, and there is an urgent need for new ways to treat and control surface infections"

"New antibiotics tend to have short shelf lives, as the bacteria they attack quickly become resistant. Many large pharmaceutical companies have abandoned antibiotic production because of the difficulty of recovering costs. Developing effective alternatives could therefore save many lives."

Link to bees dying:
http://www.inquisitr.com/206612/honey-bees-dying-from-corn-insecticides/

Link to article on Monsanto
http://www.opednews.com/articles/2/Is-Monsanto-s-Weedkiller-C-by-Sayer-Ji-120307-719.html

Link to article from vanity fair called "Monsanto's Harvest of Fear"
http://www.vanityfair.com/politi

"Let me repeat this voting for the Republicans is to be voting against the environment and we will be putting our kids and grand kids at risk."
Jeff Carlson

WAR: Never ending

"Mankind must put an end to war before war puts an end to mankind."
John F. Kennedy

"In the councils of government, we must guard against the acquisition of unwarranted influence, whether sought or unsought, by the military-industrial complex. The potential for the disastrous rise of misplaced power exists and will persist."
Dwight D. Eisenhower

War none of us want it but sometimes it must happen.

In 2012 we have a choice to continue the course with Obama, who has done a remarkable Job as Commander in Chief considering the Mess left him by the BUSH ADMIN.

The end of the war in Iraq --- Letter from the White House

"We accomplished one major change when President Obama announced that all American troops in Iraq will be home before the holidays.

With that action, the Iraq war will end. And one of the President's central promises will have been kept.

Both as Americans and as supporters of President Obama, this is something for us to reflect on, and be proud of.

The war in Iraq was a divisive, defining issue in our country for nearly nine years, and was the catalyst for many Americans to get involved in politics for the first time.

Now, thanks to the actions of this President, we can say that conflict is coming to a close.

The end of this war reflects a larger transition in our foreign policy as, in the President's words, "the tide of war is receding." The draw down in Iraq has allowed us to refocus on the fight against al Qaeda, even as we begin to bring troops home from Afghanistan. And of course, this week also marked the definitive end of the Qaddafi regime in Libya.

These outcomes are an example of what happens when a leader sets a plan and sees it through. In the last campaign, the President committed to getting American troops home while leaving behind a stable and secure Iraq. You rallied around that vision, and now that promise has been fulfilled.

 We want to thank the more than 1 million Americans who have served in Iraq, and all those who worked to make this possible."
President Barrack Obama

"Those folks don't have a lot of responsibilities,"
Obama said of his Republican challengers.

"They're not commander in chief. And when I see the casualness with which some of these folks talk about war, I'm reminded of the costs involved... This is not a game. And there's nothing casual about it."
Barack Obama, President

"If we don't end war, war will end us."
H. G. Wells author of War of the Worlds . The Time Machine, The Island of Doctor Moreau, The Invisible Man, When the Sleeper Wakes, and The First Men in the Moon.

"I hate war as only a soldier who has lived it can, only as one who has seen its brutality, its futility, its stupidity."
Dwight D. Eisenhower

Make no MISTAKE if the GOP wins this November we Will be a full out WAR IN IRAN. This war may never end once it is started and that would be fine with the Members of the Party of Scrooge.

Listen to the GOP and they are pounding the drums to WAR. They are using the Media to tell us that IRAN will have a NUKE soon all those stories sound just like what they did to get us in the ILLEGAL War in IRAN using the media to pound WMD.

Based on Real intelligence they may have a Nuke sometime around 2020, but not if we continue to seek out peaceful solutions.

'Quite Far To The Right': Meet Mitt Romney's Foreign Policy Team

By Zack Beauchamp and Ali Gharib on Jul 25, 2012

Mitt Romney turned attention to his foreign policy this week, with a largely substance-free and fact-challenged speech on Tuesday and a European tour that will eventually take him to Israel. While Romney has gone to great lengths to avoid talking national security, it's no secret that neither Romney nor his advisers appear capable of outlining a clear vision of a Romney administration's foreign policy. What little specifics we do hear sound suspiciously like the Obama administration's positions. So for those wondering what a Romney presidency might mean for U.S. troops and diplomats, there's not much to go on.

But what's troublesome about Romney on foreign policy is what's cooking behind the scenes. Gen. Colin Powell recently complained that Romney's foreign policy team is "quite far to the right." Indeed, veterans of the Bush/Cheney administration "pepper" Romney's foreign policy team and the so-called "Cheney-ites" are reportedly winning the presumptive GOP presidential nominee's ear. Here's an in depth look at some of the key advisers a President Romney will hear from on foreign policy and what we might come to expect in a Romney administration:

JOHN BOLTON

Before advising Romney, Amb. John Bolton served briefly as U.S. ambassador to the U.N. under a recess appointment — awkward from the start because of his lifelong disdain for anything multilateral. After leaving government and taking up a position at the American Enterprise Institute, he turned on the Bush administration for not being hawkish enough on Iran. It's a note he's been striking since as a Fox contributor, sometime presidential candidate, and frequent guest on right-wing conspiracy theorists' radio shows. He cheers for negotiations with Iran to fail, a position that supports his "default setting" of wanting to bomb Iran for any old reason even though he has admitted it might not work. Ominously, Bolton even once suggested a nuclear attack against Iran.

ELIOT COHEN

Just months after the war in Afghanistan began, Eliot Cohen — who "was closely affiliated with the circle of hawks who surrounded Vice President Dick Cheney" — was agitating for a war in Iraq, calling it the "big prize." As a co-founder of the Project for A New American Century, a neoconservative pressure organization critical to the development of the Iraq War, Cohen helped push the case for toppling Saddam. Though critical of the execution of the Iraq War, Cohen appears to have drawn only the most limited of conclusions, as he was seen as recently as 2009 making the case for a new war in Iran.

COFER BLACK

The Daily Beast described former C.I.A. officer Cofer Black as "Mitt Romney's trusted envoy to the dark side": "he often acts as the campaign's in-house intelligence officer." When the two first linked up during Romney's first campaign, Black still had his position as a vice chairman of the controversial security contractor known then as Blackwater. In 2007, Romney refused to rule out torture of terrorism suspects, and said he'd have to consult with Black about it. Black led the C.I.A. counterterror shop when the harsh interrogations were carried out and he took the lead on President Bush's secret rendition program. His speakers' bureau bio says Black "conceived, planned and led the CIA's war in Afghanistan." In a history of the C.I.A., Tim Weiner wrote that Black was "the man who vowed to bring Osama bin Laden's head to George W. Bush on a pike and did not make good on that promise."

WALID PHARES

When you're too controversial for Congressman Peter King's hearings on terrorism among American Muslims, that ought to be a warning flag for any prospective employers. Yet Walid Phares, a Lebanese Christian with a long history of involvement in violent militias back home, is prominently listed as a "special adviser" in official Romney campaign literature. Investigations into Phares' role in the brutal Lebanese Civil War suggests he was personally responsible for infusing Christian theology into the official ideology of the sectarian Lebanese Forces, an important fighting group in the war. Phares also has numerous links with the Islamophobic anti-Sharia movement.

MICHAEL HAYDEN

One might think Michael Hayden, who led both the CIA and the NSA at different points under George W. Bush, might be a calming influence: he has publicly warned about the consequences of a strike on Iran. However, Hayden is one of the most vigorous and defenders of torture, although accurately describing the practice he helped implement clearly makes him uncomfortable. Despite the overwhelming evidence that torture isn't an effective means of getting intelligence and the simple truth of its moral repugnance, Hayden continues to defend the practice, comparing those who agree with the expert consensus to birthers and truthers. In office, Hayden demonstrated a clear track record of covering up the facts about Bush-era torture.

DAN SENOR

A number of Romney's advisers who rose to prominence defending the Iraq war and its conduct, but none quite as much as Dan Senor. Currently the cofounder of a neoconservative pressure group, Senor was the spokesman for the U.S. Coalition Provisional Authority in Iraq, where he painted a rosy picture of the occupation, even once telling reporters, "Well, off the record, Paris is burning. But on the record, security and stability are returning to Iraq." Even after he was done, he continued to work toward improving the optics of the occupation gone awry. That approach carried over to debates about attacking Iran, where, as part of a Romney campaign call, he suggested the administration should not openly discuss consequences of a strike.

MAX BOOT

Max Boot has a remarkably consistent standard of advocating for war, even by neoconservative standards. In October of 2001, Boot called for "America to embrace its imperial role," jauntily proclaiming that "Afghanistan and other troubled lands today cry out for the sort of enlightened foreign administration once provided by self-confident Englishmen in jodhpurs and pith helmets." Though one might think he would want to downplay those remarks today, Boot recently decided he got it entirely right, only wishing "policymakers in the Bush administration had listened." Boot took an astonishingly rosy view of the ease of the Iraq War, suggesting it would only "require a long-term commitment of at least 60,000 to 75,000 soldiers." Today, Boot can be found advocating for (one presumes simultaneously) staying in Afghanistan, intervening in Syria, and bombing Iran.

ERIC EDELMAN

A former Cheney aide and Bush Ambassador to Turkey, Eric Edelman follows in his bosses' hawkish footsteps, recently suggesting that a war with Iran is the only possible alternative to an unpalatable world with an Iranian bomb. Romney recently used Edelman to attack Obama on leaking classified information, an awkward choice of spokesperson given that Edelman "originally suggested the idea to [Scooter] Libby to start leaking information about Joe Wilson's trip to Niger" when he worked for the convicted felon.

I used the Article written by By Zack Beauchamp and Ali Gharib, because it so well shows us why we need to FEAR a ROMNEY as President, because War is all you will get from these people.

There are other WARS going on that do not get much attention: War of Drugs, is one and that we need to think about and END because it is nothing more than a way to fill the Corporate Prisons.

"Anything with War attached to it has one Common denominator the GOP/ Party of Scrooge. WAR IS MONEY to the GOP."
Jeff Carlson

Labor and the attack on working Americans

Workers rights --- this is a all out war on the Middle Class.
The Party of Scrooge wants to end MIN wage, end Protection at the work place, end child labor laws, end age, gender and race protection and basically become a third world country.

The Supreme Court is going to play a huge ROLL on this -- if the Republicans win, all of what I wrote, will happen. They are talking about putting kids to work.

**"Let the workers organize. Let the toilers assemble.
Let their crystallized voice proclaim their injustices
and demand their privileges. Let all thoughtful citizens
sustain them, for the future of Labor is the future of America."**
John L. Lewis, President of the United Mine Workers of America (UMW) from 1920 to 1960.

"Without labor nothing prospers."
Sophocles

"It was the labor movement that helped secure so much of what we take for granted today. The 40-hour work week, the minimum wage, family leave, health insurance, Social Security, Medicare, retirement plans. The cornerstones of the middle-class security all bear the union label."
Barack Obama

Labor --- Workers Rights

The Republican Party wants to:
End the Organization of Unions,
End MIN wage,
End Protection at the work place,
End Child labor laws,
End Age, Gender and Race protection.
Basically become a third world country.

"In our glorious fight for civil rights, we must guard against being fooled by false slogans, as 'right-to-work.'   It provides no 'rights' and no 'works.' Its purpose is to destroy labor unions and the freedom of collective bargaining... We demand this fraud be stopped."
 Martin Luther King, Jr. quotes (American Baptist Minister and Civil-Rights Leader. 1929-1968)

The compensation penalty of "right-to-work" laws
By Elise Gould and Heidi Shierholz | February 17, 2011

The simple reality is that RTW laws undermine the resources that help workers bargain for better wages and benefits.

We find the following:
Wages in right-to-work states are 3.2% lower than those in non-RTW states, after controlling for a full complement of individual demographic and socioeconomic variables as well as state macroeconomic indicators. Using the average wage in non-RTW states as the base ($22.11), the average full-time, full-year worker in an RTW state makes about $1,500 less annually than a similar worker in a non-RTW state.
The rate of employer-sponsored pensions is 4.8 percentage points lower in RTW states, using the full complement of control variables in our regression model. If

workers in non-RTW states were to receive pensions at this lower rate, 3.8 million fewer workers nationally would have pensions.

This briefing paper provides the most comprehensive study to date of the relationship between RTW status and compensation. Using a full set of explanatory variables, including state-level controls, it is clear that our analysis stands apart as being more rigorous than others of this type.

Again in 2012 we have Choices Lets not make the mistake we did in 2010.

Here is a Poem written so many years ago talking about the Nazi's taking over Germany and there are many similarities to the Current Republican Party and the Take Over of America.

"When the Nazis came for the communists,
I remained silent;
I was not a communist.

When they locked up the social democrats,
I remained silent;
I was not a social democrat.

When they came for the trade unionists,
I did not speak out;
I was not a trade unionist.

When they came for the Jews,
I remained silent;
I wasn't a Jew.

When they came for me,
there was no one left to speak out."

Martin Niemöller

Voting Rights

Voter suppression:
Being done in 34 Republican states will stop as many as 5 million people from voting. We must go all out to make sure these people have ID's and are registered -- the party of Scrooge will be going all out to stop people from voting -- that is reason enough to throw them out of office.

"Voting is the most precious right of every citizen, and we have a moral obligation to ensure the integrity of our voting process."
Hillary Clinton

"There has never been in my lifetime, since we got rid of the poll tax and all the Jim Crow burdens on voting, the determined effort to limit the franchise that we see today."
Former President Bill Clinton said of Voter ID laws at the 2011 Campus Progress National Conference

Voter Suppression is what the Republican Party is all about.

Millions of Americans could be turned away at the polls in 2012, according to a Campus Progress survey of the Voter ID laws making They're way through state legislatures across the country.

Seventeen states have passed restrictive Voter ID laws since 2010.

The voters most affected by these new requirements are students, seniors, people of color, and people of low-income.

We must Help get these people registered and get them Proper ID's and then Vote in 2012 the people that want to suppress the Voters, Out of Office.

WOMEN ISSUES

Women Issues ---
Quote from Kathleen Turner Kathleen Turner, PFAW Supporter & PFAW Foundation Board Member

"This year, we've seen leaders and candidates at every level in the Republican Party wage shocking attacks on women and their position in this country. They have gone from claiming that victims of "legitimate" rape rarely get pregnant, to implying that women should prepare for rape the way one prepares for a flat tire in their car.

The GOP has attacked women's use of contraception. They've attacked funding for family planning and the health clinics women rely on. They've failed to renew a comprehensive Violence against Women Act to protect all women from violence. And they've failed to pass the Paycheck Fairness Act, designed to close the pay gap between women and men."

Their attack on Women is relentless and they seem to only care about the Fetus because once baby born they want nothing to do with you.

This is a EMAIL that was sent to me had no origin but should be read by all:

WOMEN'S RIGHT TO VOTE

A little history -- in the middle of Convention season

I got this as a EMAIL and it had some wonderful Pics to go with it but I thought the message will give you a IDEA of what women had to do in order to vote.

This refers to women but really applies to everyone. Become knowledgeable and vote.

Our mothers and grand mothers who lived only 90 years ago.

Remember it was not until 1920 that women were granted the right to go to the polls and vote.

The women were innocent and defenseless, but they were jailed nonetheless for picketing the White House, carrying signs asking for the vote.

And by the end of the night, they were barely alive. Forty prison guards wielding clubs and their warden's blessing went on a rampage against the 33 women wrongly convicted of 'obstructing sidewalk traffic.'

(Lucy Burns)
They beat Lucy Burns, chained her hands to the cell bars above her head and left her hanging for the night, bleeding and gasping for air.

(Dora Lewis)
They hurled Dora Lewis into a dark cell, smashed her head against an iron bed and knocked her out cold. Her cell mate, Alice Cosu, thought Lewis was dead and suffered a heart attack. Additional affidavits describe the guards grabbing, dragging, beating, choking, slamming, pinching, twisting and kicking the women.

Thus unfolded the 'Night of Terror' on Nov. 15, 1917, when the warden at the Occoquan Workhouse in Virginia ordered his guards to teach a lesson to the suffragists imprisoned there because they dared to picket Woodrow Wilson's White House for the right to vote. For weeks, the women's only water came from an open pail. Their food--all of it colorless slop--was infested with worms.

(Alice Paul)
When one of the leaders, Alice Paul, embarked on a hunger strike, they tied her to a chair, forced a tube down her throat and poured liquid into her until she vomited. She was tortured like this for weeks until word was smuggled out to the press.

So, refresh MY memory. Some women won't vote this year because - Why, exactly? We have carpool duties? We have to get to work? Our vote doesn't matter? It's raining?

Mrs. Pauline Adams in the prison garb she wore while serving a 60 day sentence.

Last week, I went to a sparsely attended screening of HBO's new movie 'Iron Jawed Angels.' It is a graphic depiction of the battle these women waged so that I could pull the curtain at the polling booth and have my say. I am ashamed to say I needed the reminder.

Miss **Edith Ainge**, of Jamestown, New York
All these years later, voter registration is still my passion. But the actual act of voting had become less personal for me, more rote. Frankly, voting often felt more like an obligation than a privilege. Sometimes it was inconvenient.

(Berthe Arnold, CSU graduate)
My friend Wendy, who is my age and studied women's history, saw the HBO movie, too. When she stopped by my desk to talk
about it, she looked angry. She was--with herself. 'One thought kept coming back to me as I watched that movie,' she said. 'What would those women think of the way I use, or don't use, my right to vote? All of us take it for granted now, not just younger women, but those of us who did seek to learn.' The right to vote, she said, had become valuable to her 'all over again.'

HBO released the movie on video and DVD. I wish all history, social studies and government teachers would include the movie in their curriculum I want it shown on Bunco/Bingo night, too, and anywhere else women gather. I realize this isn't our usual idea of socializing, but we are not voting in the numbers that we should be, and I think a little shock therapy is in order.

Conferring over ratification of the 19th Amendment to the U.S. Constitution at National Woman's Party headquarters, Jackson Place, Washington, D.C.
Mrs. Lawrence Lewis, Mrs. Abby Scott Baker, Anita Pollitzer, Alice Paul, Florence Boeckel, Mabel Vernon

It is jarring to watch Woodrow Wilson and his cronies try to persuade a psychiatrist to declare Alice Paul insane so that she could be permanently institutionalized. And it is inspiring to watch the doctor refuse. Alice Paul was strong, he said, and brave. That didn't make her crazy.

The doctor admonished the men: **'Courage in women is often mistaken for insanity.'**

Please, if you are so inclined, pass this on to all the women you know. We need to get out and vote and use this right that was fought so hard for by these very courageous women.

Whether you vote democratic, republican or independent party - remember to vote.

The Email had some wonderful Pictures to go with it but because of time restraints, I just wanted to share the message.

IMMIGRATION

Immigration --- Mitt Romney wants to adopt the Arizona Immigration laws of show me your papers, all over the country. A reminder that is exactly what the Nazi's did as they took over Germany, but that is no surprise they have been patterning their whole party after the take over of Germany oh so many years ago, fascism is alive and well in the name of Republicans.

Note to all the man who wrote the Arizona laws is going to head a Romney's Immigration department. NOT acceptable at all.

"These are things that will happen if we as a PARTY do not stand as one come 2012. Nothing would shock the Party of Scrooge and Karl Rove more than all of us that are Democrats ignore the MEDIA BLITZ and say we are VOTING and VOTING DEMOCRAT and that includes OBAMA."
Jeff Carlson

Grover Norquist

"We are trying to change the tones in the state capitals - and turn them toward bitter nastiness and partisanship."
 Grover Norquist president of Americans for Tax Reform (ATR)

"Tyrants have always some slight shade of virtue; they support the laws before destroying them"
 Voltaire (French Philosopher and Writer. One of the greatest of all French authors, 1694-1778)

Who is Grover Norquist? What is Tyranny? Are they the same?

Norquist wants to impeach Obama if he does not extend the BUSH
Tax cuts for the upper 1%.

238 House members and 41 Senators have taken the pledge. Including Romney and Ryan. It is a disgrace and sad.

On the state level, 13 governors and 1249 state legislators
have taken the pledge. Giving their allegiance to Norquist
over their allegiance to the people who elected them.

This is treason by the constitution but the only ones that can call them on it is the members of the House and that will never happen.

Every single one of these elected officials have SOLD out America to the Devil and Greed.

Student Loans Lets FIX IT

Here is what needs to be done:

1. All Federal Student Loans would be paid off:

The total outstanding student loan debt reached $870 billion last year, according to the Federal Reserve Bank of New York. However, the new Consumer Financial Protection Bureau estimates that the debt topped $1 trillion, more than the amount in credit card loans or auto loans last year.

2. We pay for this by making Wall Street pay back some of the cash they stole from the American People. Each of the 5 leading Banks will be responsible for 1/5 of the Debt.
NO OPTIONS on this.

a. Any one working at a company that was bailed out and were making more than 1 million dollars have to pay 10% on Money Made the year of the Bail Out.

b. From this day on we charge a small fee on all trades generating enough cash to pay all federal student loans.

Douste-Blazey laid out the basics: "A tax of just 0.05 percent levied on each stock, bond, derivative or currency transaction would be aimed at financial institutions' casino-style trading, which helped precipitate the economic crisis. Because these markets are so vast, the fee could raise hundreds of billions of dollars a year globally for cash-strapped governments and could increase development aid."

Link to article about Trades:
http://www.metroactive.com/features/how-to-fix-the-economy.html

c. A 50% tax on all profits made from OIL and OTHER Speculating -- We need to stop these crooks from manipulating markets.

3. How it works for Students:

a. Old loans would just be wiped off the books giving the largest stimulus in the history of this country.

b. All new Federal loans would have some obligations:

Students would need to have passing grades (if not they are responsible for loans on classes failed).

c. They would owe the government some sort of service depending on the amounts of loans needed. This can be set up --- Peace Core, Military, Work Programs and many other things that would benefit this country.

4. This would be a stimulus that would jump start the economy making things better for all. Yes it would be better for some than others but the point is we need to move forward in this country. The stimulus would more than generate enough money to make sure we are not adding to deficits.

5. Why pick on Wall Street, maybe I do not need to say this, most of them belong in jail, so lets get some blood out them, seems they only know one thing, "GREED IS GOOD and people do not count". Lets make them say ouch a bit, and lets face it, most would not feel this at all.

"Education is a better safeguard of liberty than a standing army."
Edward Everett (April 11, 1794 – January 15, 1865) was an American politician and educator from Massachusetts.

"Education is not preparation for life; education is life itself."
John Dewey (October 20, 1859 – June 1, 1952) was an American philosopher, psychologist and educational reformer whose ideas have been influential in education and social reform.

"I read Shakespeare and the Bible, and I can shoot dice. That's what I call a liberal education."
Tallulah Bankhead (January 31, 1902 – December 12, 1968) was an American actress of the stage and screen.

"We have an obligation and a responsibility to be investing in our students and our schools. We must make sure that people who have the grades, the desire and the will, but not the money, can still get the best education possible."
Barack Obama

STUDENT LOANS:
Vote Republican you will get 6.8%

The Ryan bill fixes Student Loans at 6.8% not good for our future students.

Romney , was talking about how great the Ryan Bill is and he supports it fully. Read Below about BONER and SO many other Republicans have been LYING about the same. Remember this, they all signed the RYAN BILL and that fixes the Student Loan at 6.8%

What do the Republicans do when they are on the losing side of everything ---- THEY LIE --- good article spelling it out

Excerpt from the Article:
Setting the groundwork for the GOP congressional capitulation to President Obama's insistence that interest rates not be raised on college loans, Speaker John Boehner announced today that the House will vote to keep the rates at the current level and will pay for it from a 'slush fund' in the Affordable Care Act.

In making his announcement, Boehner claimed there was never any intent on the GOP's part to raise the rates on student loans and that President Obama had simply manufactured this disagreement to score political points with young voters and their families.

I wonder, then, how the Speaker would explains the provision in the Ryan Budget — passed last month by all the Republicans in the House but ten — that doubles the student loan rate to 6.8 percent on July 1, 2012?

And that Obamacare 'slush fund' the Speaker intends to raid to pay for holding the line on the student loans?

It turns out, the fund in jeopardy was created in the Affordable Care Act to screen women for breast and cervical cancer in addition to providing funds for the treatment of children with birth defects.

This, apparently, is Speaker Boehner's idea of a slush fund.

Link to Article about LIES
http://www.forbes.com/sites/rickungar/2012/04/25/john-boehner-flat-out-lies-on-student-loans-as-he-capitulates-to-obama/

DARE TO CALL IT TREASON

ON JANUARY 20, 2009, IN A SECRET MEETING, THESE REPUBLICAN CONGRESSIONAL POLICYMAKERS CONSPIRED TO SABOTAGE, UNDERMINE, AND IF NECESSARY, DESTROY THE U.S. ECONOMY, IN ORDER TO PREVENT RE-ELECTION OF A DEMOCRATICALLY ELECTED PRESIDENT

Rep. Paul Ryan (R-WI)
Rep. Eric Cantor (R-VA)
Rep. Kevin McCarthy (R-CA)
Sen. Jim DeMint (SC-R)
Sen. Tom Coburn (OK-R)
Sen. John Ensign (NV-R)
Rep. Pete Sessions (R-TX)
Rep. Jeb Hensarling (R-TX)
Rep. Pete Hoekstra (R-MI)
Rep. Dan Lungren (R-CA)
Sen. Jon Kyl (AZ-R)
Sen. Bob Corker (TN-R) Non-lawmakers present:
Newt Gingrich - Former GOP Speaker
Frank Luntz - GOP Strategist
Fred Barnes, Journalist

During the swearing-in ceremony of President Obama in January 2009, 15 Republican policy makers were in a somber mood as they gathered in a private dining room at the Caucus Room in Washington, an upscale restaurant where a New York strip steak costs $51. They were there at the invitation of Republican strategist Frank Luntz, who organized the dinner and sent out the invitations. The purpose of the secret meeting; to plot and scheme and craft the demise of an Obama second term..

This secret meeting included right-wing journalist Fred Barnes. In addition to Luntz and Barnes, the other non-lawmaker present was former speaker and presidential candidate, Newt Gingrich, who had been forced to resign from Congress in disgrace. A detailed account of who was present at the dinner on that January 20 night and the plan they worked out to bring down Obama is provided by Robert Draper in 'Do Not Ask What Good We Do: Inside the US House of Representatives', which hit the bookshelves in April of 2012.

The dinner table was set at Luntz's request so everyone could see one another and talk freely. The session lasted four hours and by the end the somber mood had lifted: they had conceived a plan. They would take back the House in November 2010, which they did, and use it as a spear to mortally wound Obama in 2011 and take back the Senate and White House in 2012, "We've got to challenge them on every single bill and challenge them on every single campaign.", insisted Rep.Kevin McCarthy.)R-CA)

At the end of the meeting, Gingrich declared, "You will remember this day. You'll remember this as the day the seeds of 2012 were sown."

"The single most important thing we want to achieve is for President Obama to be a one-term president."
2010 quote from Senate minority leader, Mitch McConnell:

The agreed upon plan was for the entire Republican electorate to unilaterally oppose, delay, and reject, everything proposed by the President, regardless of the consequences to the country they were elected to serve and the people they were elected to represent. Moderate Republicans who voiced their opposition to the plan were told in no uncertain terms that they would be targeted for removal by their own party, and replaced with radical, far-right conservatives, who would have no objection to embracing the newly devised hard line strategy.

"The New York Times has calculated that 78% of the more moderate half of the Republican caucus in the Senate in 2007 has left office, compared with just 39% of the conservatives. After the next election, the few that remain will be more fearful than ever of a primary challenge from the right. That is a recipe, as Mr Lugar put it, for "an unrelenting partisan mindset" marked by "reflexive votes for a rejectionist orthodoxy and rigid opposition to the actions and proposals of the other party". The results will be frustrating not just for the tea party, but for everyone."

Republicans have opposed a lion's share of stimulus measures that once they supported, such as a payroll tax break, which they grudgingly embraced earlier in the year. Even unemployment insurance, a relatively uncontroversial tool for helping those in an economic downturn, has been consistently held up by Republicans or used as a bargaining chip for more tax cuts. Ten years ago, prominent conservatives were loudly making the case for fiscal stimulus to get the economy going; today, they treat such ideas like they're the plague. Republicans have also upbraided Ben Bernanke, head of the Federal Reserve, for even considering policies that focus on growing the economy and creating jobs. And then, there is the fact that since the original stimulus bill passed in February of 2009, Republicans have made practically no effort to draft comprehensive job creation legislation. Instead, they continue to pursue austerity policies, which reams of historical data suggest harms economic recovery and does little to create jobs. In fact, since taking control of the House of Representatives in 2011, Republicans have proposed hardly a single major jobs bill that didn't revolve, in some way, around their one-stop solution for all the nation's economic problems: more tax cuts for the wealthy. Republican austerity policies are not only harming America's present, but also imperiling its future.

Frank I. Luntz is an American political consultant, pollster, and Republican Party strategist. His most recent work has been with the Fox News Channel as a frequent commentator and analyst, as well as running focus groups after presidential debates. Frank Luntz specializes in Propaganda. An avid student of the propaganda tactics of the Third Reich's Joseph Goebbels, Luntz is skilled in the politics of division. Like Goebbels, he advocated the deliberate spread of hate, lies and fear, in order to gain control.

"I focus on words that cause people to change their minds, change their behavior even change their attitudes." ~Frank Luntz 3/20/11 in interview with Matt Lauer

In the post World War II era, word-crafting, or political double-speak, as we know it, was made famous by the prescient author George Orwell's book "1984", and his descriptions on political speech from his essays Politics and the English Language. Although there is no mention of Doublespeak in Nineteen Eighty-Four, it has been argued that the term is a combination of two concepts - Doublethink and Newspeak, which are original to his work. Orwell wrote, "unscrupulous politicians, advertisers, religionists, and other double speakers of whatever stripe continue to abuse language for manipulative purposes".

Minister of Propaganda Goebbels wrote: "If you tell a lie big enough and keep repeating it, people will eventually come to believe it. The lie can be maintained only for such time as the State can shield the people from the political, economic and/or military consequences of the lie. It thus becomes vitally important for the State to use all of its powers to repress dissent, for the truth is the mortal enemy of the lie, and thus by extension, the truth is the greatest enemy of the State." "It would not be impossible to prove with sufficient repetition and a psychological understanding of the people concerned that a square is in fact a circle. They are mere words, and words can be molded until they clothe ideas and disguise."

GOP strategist Frank Luntz agreed with Goebbels philosophy and opined that the vast majority of Americans, in particular the less educated, who are politely termed "Under-Informed Voters" could easily be persuaded to accept what Republicans would put forth as their "New Reality". A certain segment of the masses could also be convinced, for example, that legislation specifically implemented to benefit them or to benefit their planet, was instead being forced upon them in order to do them harm and restrict their freedom.

Media coverage of an issue can play a particularly important part in shaping political reality. The Fox "News" channel, for example, is primarily a right wing propaganda medium, employed to reinforce the GOP's political stratagem.

Doublespeak is language that deliberately disguises, distorts, or reverses the meaning of words. Doublespeak may take the form of euphemisms (e.g., "downsizing" for layoffs, "servicing the target" for bombing, making the truth less unpleasant, without denying its nature. It may also be deployed as intentional ambiguity, or reversal of meaning (for example, naming a state of war "peace"). In such cases, doublespeak disguises the nature of the truth, producing a communication bypass.

Luntz's plan was to use words that were basically the opposite of factual descriptions.

These are a few of his recommendations:

Don't say "oil drilling." Say "energy independence."

Don't say "inheritance tax." Say "death tax."

Don't say "Capitalism." Say "Economic Freedom."

Don't say that the government 'taxes the rich.' Say Government "takes from the rich."

Don't admit Lobbyists are Collective Bargainers for Corporations. Say "Union Collective Bargaining steals your tax dollars."

Don't say "healthcare reform." Say "government takeover."

Don't say "Public workers." Call them "Government workers."

Don't tell Occupy Wall Street "you don't give a shit." Say "I get it."

Don't tell struggling Americans "you're on your own." Say "I get it."

Don't tell Occupy Wall Street "you should protest Wall Street." Say "You should occupy the White House."

A political action committee (PAC) is any organization in the United States that campaigns for or against political candidates, ballot initiatives or legislation. At the federal level, an organization becomes a PAC when it receives or spends more than $1,000 for the purpose of influencing a federal election, according to the Federal Election Campaign Act. At the state level, an organization becomes a PAC according to the state's election laws. Go-to words in the Republican Super PAC formula are "liberty," "freedom" and "values." With the passage of Citizens United, corporations have effectively been given a green light to purchase elections.

As of September 01, 2012, 819 groups organized as Super PACs have reported total receipts of over THREE HUNDRED FORTY NINE MILLION dollars ($349,323,435.00) and total independent expenditures of $216,845,528 of that occurred within the first eight months of the 2012 cycle.

Republican SuperPACs employed a Luntz naming strategy:

Below: A handful of Republican SuperPACS, referencing just a few of their sponsors: Raised to date:
Restore Our Future, Inc. is bankrolled by hotel and home developers, Wall Street investment firms, coal companies and a few super-rich guys who are chiefly interested in their own futures. Casino magnate Sheldon Adelson has said he is willing to donate up to one hundred million dollars. Adelson is currently under investigation for violation of the Foreign Corrupt Practices Act. He would like the investigation to go away. Harold Simons, Dallas businessman, donated $800,000. Texas homebuilder Bob Perry contributed $13.9 million to super PACs. Perry is one of the most prolific donors in contemporary political history. He was a major backer of Swift Boat Veterans for Truth, the outside group that helped torpedo John Kerry's presidential campaign in 2004. Perry's net worth has been estimated at around $650 million. Perry has given $8 million to Restore Our Future (supporting Romney). $89,654,176
American Crossroads is a tool of Karl Rove (Bush's Brain). Harold Simmons, the octogenarian Dallas businessman, combined with his wife Annette and his company, Contran Corp., to donate $19,205,000 to super PACs. Simmons is listed in Forbes magazine as the 33rd richest person in America with a net worth of $9.3 billion. Simmons and Contran donated $13 million to American Crossroads. Texas homebuilder Bob Perry a major backer of Swift Boat Veterans for Truth, the outside group that helped torpedo John Kerry's presidential campaign in 200 donated $4.5 million to American Crossroads, $47,340,973
Winning Our Future originally supporting Newt Gingrich, was backed by Sheldon Adelson, the Las Vegas casino magnate. He and his family have combined to give $37.75 million to super PACs in the 2012 election cycle. At first, Adelson pumped money into Winning Our Future, the super PAC supporting

Newt Gingrich, but now he is funding groups backing Mitt Romney and congressional Republicans. Adelson is ranked on the Forbes list of the richest Americans at number eight, with $21.5 billion in net worth. Harold Simons, Dallas businessman, donated one million dollars to Winning Our Future. $23,921,215

Club for Growth Action is the 8th largest giver to political campaigns. The purpose of this mega-billionaire funded shadow group is to elect legislators who can convince "low-information voters" that the "economy is too fragile" to raise taxes on the rich. The Club is primarily a conduit for its bigger givers to give to "outside" organizations via the Club's 527, then funnel the money directly to aid candidates, either with attack ads, or with supportive position ads, that could not be donated due to the limits in individual giving directly to a candidate. Notable "members" include John W. Childs, one of the wealthiest Bostonians, managing billions for Insurance companies, Jackson T. Stephens of Little Rock, Arkansas, is the CEO of a wholesale drugs and sundries company, Mr. Richard E. Uihlein, the Co-Founder and CEO of the packaging materials giant, Ronald M. (Ronnie) Cameron, whose company Mountaire Corp in North Little Rock, one of the top companies in Arkansas, The Cato Institute is the well known Libertarian think-tank funded by the Koch Brothers, and among others, the late Roger Milliken, his trusts and/or foundations, join the Dead Billionaires Club which funds Tea Party extremism from beyond the grave. Thomas L. Rhodes, Chairman and political editor of the conservative publication The National Review and a former employee of Goldman Sachs is the Chairman of two investment companies based in Denver, Colorado. He sits on a number of ultra-conservative boards including the Heritage Foundation, a think-tank founded with money from the Dead Billionaires Club. MORE $13,252,084

The Red White and Blue Fund, is backed mainly by mutual fund manager Foster Friess who was supporting Rick Santorum. Friess is now reportedly considering major contributions to American Crossroads. $8,517,926

Make US Great Again, originally supporting Rick Perry, is backed mainly from energy company executives. Harold Simons, Dallas businessman, donated one million dollars. $5,607,881

Freedom Works for America - backed by David Koch (Koch Industries). Dick Armey, Jack Kemp and C. Boyden Gray, William Bennett, former Secretary of HUD Jack Kemp, former Ambassador Jeane J. Kirkpatrick, former Representative Vin Weber, and Steve Forbes, Freedom Works helps run the Tea Party Patriots, In 2011, Freedom Works launched a Super PAC. The stated purpose of this PAC is to "empower the leaderless, decentralized community of the tea party movement as it continues its hostile takeover of the GOP establishment." Activities of Freedom Works for America include lobbying for removal of CEO's whose business practices are considered "green friendly" and environmentally sound. Freedom Works endorsed 114 candidates for federal office in 2010, of whom seventy won election. $5,385,201

SOURCES:
http://www.dailykos.com/story/2012/06/08/1098434/-Eric-Cantor-Paul-Ryan-Kevin-McCarthy-Plot-To-Sabotage-US-Economy-with-Frank-Luntz
http://www.alaskadispatch.com/article/who-funds-super-pac-fec-looks-powerful-influence
http://www.miamiherald.com/2012/06/23/2863824/super-pacs-who-comes-up-with-those.html
http://www.opensecrets.org/pacs/superpacs.php
http://www.guardian.co.uk/commentisfree/2012/jun/09/did-republicans-deliberately-crash-us-economy
http://www.economist.com/blogs/democracyinamerica/2012/05/tea-party
http://www.vanityfair.com/online/wolcott/2012/03/The-Conspiracy-to-Commit-Legislative-Constipation

TREASON AND THE HISTORY OF THE REPUBLICAN PARTY

CONNECTING THE DOTS NOT HARD TO SEE HOW SICK THEY ARE

Nixon in 1968 committed treason, won the election because of it;

On May 14, 1973, Walt W. Rostow, who had been national security adviser during some of the darkest days of the Vietnam War, typed a three-page "memorandum for the record" summarizing a secret file that his former boss, President Lyndon Johnson, had amassed on what may have been Richard Nixon's dirtiest trick, the sabotaging of Vietnam peace talks to win the 1968 election.

Rostow reflected, too, on what effect LBJ's public silence may have had on the then-unfolding Watergate scandal. As Rostow composed his memo in spring 1973, President Nixon's Watergate cover-up was unraveling. Just two weeks earlier, Nixon had fired White House counsel John Dean and accepted the resignations of two top aides, H.R. Haldeman and John Ehrlichman.

http://consortiumnews.com/2012/03/03/lbjs-x-file-on-nixons-treason/

Reagan committed treason in 1980, won the election because of it

Palestinian president Yasir Arafat has joined the growing list of world leaders to confirm that Ronald Reagan's 1980 campaign did try to disrupt President Carter's negotiations to free 52 Americans then held hostage in Iran.

Arafat shared the secret with Carter 15 years after the end of Carter's presidency, according to an article by historian Douglas Brinkley in the fall issue of the scholarly journal Diplomatic History. Arafat informed Carter about the Republican sabotage efforts during a private meeting between the two men last Jan. 22 at Arafat's bunker-headquarters in Gaza City.

"There is something I want to tell you," Arafat said, addressing Carter. "You should know that in 1980 the Republicans approached me with an arms deal [for the Palestine Liberation Organization] if I could arrange to keep the hostages in Iran until after the [U.S. presidential] election."

http://www.consortiumnews.com/archive/lost10.html

Lets look at today's Republicans:

Number one, each and every Republican has signed a pledge to Glover Norquist that they would not raise any taxes on the Rich. That is treason because the elected officials are not serving the people that elected them they are there to serve Norquist.

Number two right after the election the top members of the Republican Party got together and conspired to do everything they can to make sure the economy does not recover and they make President Obama a one term President. In his famous Quote Mitch McConnel said just that.

Folks that is treason against the President and the American People.

Now this is going on and I would not bet that behind it is the extreme Right Wing of the Republican Party looking at making the world unsafe so they can gain Political Gain

Muslims enraged over film murder U.S. ambassador to Libya

This "Arab Spring" certainly has resulted in a flowering of democracy and pluralism, just as the mainstream media told us it would. "U.S. ambassador to Libya killed in Benghazi attack," by Tamim Elyan and Omar al-Mosmari for Reuters, September 11:

http://www.jihadwatch.org/2012/09/muslims-enraged-over-film-murder-us-ambassador-to-libya.html

"Nothing coming out of the Republican Party is good for the American People and Treason, Hate and Lies can all be traced to them."
Jeff Carlson

Information you need to know

In this chapter I want to show you things we all need to know and things we will be hearing about as the campaign for the President moves along.

One thing I discovered is most Americans do not actually know about the buzz words that keep cropping up things like Socialist, Commie, Fascist and many other Political Systems.

Making Laws --- CIVICS 101

A "bill" is introduced when a member of Congress decides to create a new law. Any member of Congress can introduce a bill. Only members of the House may introduce bills that deal with taxes or spending. Before a bill can become a law, both houses of Congress must pass identical versions of the bill.

Once a bill is introduced in either house, it goes through almost the same process. Each bill is first assigned to a committee for review. The bill is tabled, or set aside, if the committee decides the bill is not worthy. The bill is sent to the entire house for debate if the committee decides the bill is worthy of further action.

If the bill passes, it is sent to the other house. A joint committee works out any differences the two houses of Congress have concerning a bill. When both houses agree on a bill, the Speaker of the House and the vice president sign it. The bill must be signed before being sent to the president.

In each two-year session, thousands of bills come before Congress. Almost twelve thousand bills were introduced in Congress in one recent session. Less than five hundred were enacted into law.

The Veto:

A bill becomes law if the president signs it. The president doesn't always wish to sign the bill. He may choose to say "no" by vetoing it. If this happens, the bill is sent back to Congress.

If two-thirds of all the members of Congress vote "yes," the bill can still become law. The bill dies when there are not enough votes to override the President. For example, when George Bush was president, Congress tried to override his vetoes thirty-six times but was successful only once.

Sometimes a president decides to do nothing. He may decide neither to sign nor veto a bill. If Congress is in session, the bill becomes law after ten days without the president's signature. Otherwise, the bill suffers a pocket veto and does not become law.

Economics 101

Demand-side Economics
A school of economic thought founded by the UK economist John Maynard Keynes (1883-1946) and developed by his followers. Its main assertion is that the aggregate demand created by households, businesses and the government and not the dynamics of free markets is the most important driving force in an economy. It further asserts that free markets (despite the assertion of 18th century Scottish economist Adam Smith and other classical economists) have no self-balancing mechanisms that lead to full employment. This has been tied to Keynesian Economics.

Keynesian economics advocates a mixed economy — predominantly private sector, but with a significant role of government and public sector — and served as the economic model during the later part of the Great Depression, World War II, and the post-war economic expansion (1945–1973), though it lost some influence following the stagflation of the 1970s.

The advent of the global financial crisis in 2008 has caused a resurgence in Keynesian thought.

Supply-side economics:

Supply-side economics is a school of macroeconomic thought that argues that economic growth can be most effectively created by lowering barriers for people to produce (supply) goods and services, such as lowering income tax and capital gains tax rates, and by allowing greater flexibility by reducing regulation. According to supply-side economics, consumers will then benefit from a greater supply of goods and services at lower prices. Typical policy recommendations of supply-side economists are lower marginal tax rates and less regulation. This is tied to Market-Oriented Economics.

Supply-side/Market-Oriented (This is the Party of Scrooge's Agenda)
Reduction in Income Tax
Reduction in Corporation Tax
Reduction in Trade Union power
Reduction/elimination of minimum wage
Reduction in Benefit allowances
Deregulation
Privatize

Understanding Economics and the two paths that we can go.

Supply Side economics lead to the Gilded Age Depression and many years later lead to the Great Depression and it has always been Demand Side Economics that has lead us back to a sane economy.

The Party of Scrooge wants to use Supply-side, that is what we saw from BUSH and it led to the destruction of our economy. Do we really want to go back to those policies?

Now we get to what I call Common sense economics and it has been called Demand economics and sometimes called Keynesian economics.

Thing is in America nothing grows unless there is a DEMAND for goods and Services. In order to have this people need to have JOBS and those Jobs have to pay a living wage.

(NOTE)
The Party of Scrooge wants to CUT WAGES and Benefits and end Minimum Wage. Not to mention put young kids to work.

To have this country working again and creating jobs we need both the Private sector and the Government to work hand in hand.

(NOTE)
Republican policies after being put in power in 2010 by using the LIE of "JOBS JOBS JOBS," have eliminated close to 2.5 million jobs. You got to wonder just how much better this country would be now with those 2.5 million people still working.

Bottom Line come this election we need to make sure we Control the House, Senate and the White House and then get on to our Progressive Agenda and put Americans back to work.

State Elections count that is where Republican Governors have laid off over 2 million people.

Quote By: Mark Twain -- The Gilded Age 1870 -- 1900

"No country can be well governed unless its citizens as a body keep religiously before their minds that they are the guardians of the law and that the law officers are only the machinery for its execution, nothing more."

Why care about the Gilded Age --- History has a way of repeating.
I see that we just might be going though our Own GILDED AGE
and the 99% be leading us or at least representing us.

In A Nutshell
The Gilded Age lasted from 1870-1900
The name came from the title of a Mark Twain book
"Gilded" means covered with gold on the outside, but not really golden on the inside
The Gilded Age was a period of rapid economic growth but also much social conflict

Key Points
Rapid economic growth generated vast wealth during the Gilded Age.
New products and technologies improved middle-class quality of life.
Industrial workers and farmers did not share in the new prosperity, working long hours in dangerous conditions for low pay.
Gilded Age politicians were largely corrupt and ineffective
Most Americans during the Gilded Age wanted political and social reforms, but they disagreed strongly on what kind of reform

Link to learn more about Gilded Age
http://www.shmoop.com/gilded-age/

The Gilded Age 1870 -- 1900

In United States history, the Gilded Age refers to the era of rapid economic and population growth in the United States during the post-Civil War and post-Reconstruction eras of the late 19th century. The term "Gilded Age" was coined by Mark Twain and Charles Dudley Warner in their book The Gilded Age: A Tale of Today. The name refers to the process of gilding an object with a superficial layer of gold and is meant to make fun of ostentatious display while playing on the term "golden age."
The Gilded Age is most famous for the creation of a modern industrial economy. During the 1870s and 1880s, the U.S. economy grew at the fastest rate in its

history, with real wages, wealth, GDP, and capital formation all increasing rapidly.

Thick national networks for transportation and communication were created. The corporation became the dominant form of business organization, and a managerial revolution transformed business operations.

The super-rich industrialists and financiers such as John D. Rockefeller, Andrew W. Mellon, Andrew Carnegie, Henry Flagler, Henry H. Rogers, J.P. Morgan, Cornelius Vanderbilt of the Vanderbilt family, and the prominent Astor family were attacked as "robber barons" by critics, who believed they cheated to get their money and lorded it over the common people. There was a small, growing labor union movement led especially by Samuel Gompers, head of the American Federation of Labor (AFL) after 1886.

The end of the Gilded Age coincided with the Panic of 1893, a deep depression, which lasted until 1897 and marked a major political realignment in the election of 1896. This productive but divisive era was followed by the Progressive Era.

POLITICS

Americans' sense of civic virtue was shocked by the scandals associated with the Reconstruction era: corrupt state governments, massive fraud in cities controlled by political machines, political payoffs to secure government contracts (especially the Crédit Mobilier of America scandal regarding the financing of the transcontinental railroad), and widespread evidence of government corruption during the Ulysses S. Grant Administration.

This corruption divided the Republican party into two different factions, The Stalwarts led by Roscoe Conkling and the Half-Breeds led by James G. Blaine. Accordingly there were widespread calls for reform, such as Civil Service Reform led by the Bourbon Democrats and Republican Mugwumps supporting Democratic reform candidates such as Grover Cleveland.

There was a sense that government intervention in the economy inevitably led to favoritism, bribery, kickbacks, inefficiency, waste, and corruption. The Bourbon Democrats led the call for a free market, low tariffs, low taxes, less spending and, in general, a Laissez-Faire (hands-off) government. They specifically denounced imperialism and overseas expansion. Many business and professional people supported this approach, although — to encourage rapid growth of industry and protect America's high wages against the low wage system in Europe — most Republicans advocated a high protective tariff. Labor activists and agrarians expressed the same spirit but focused their attacks on monopolies and railroads as unfair to the little man. Many Republicans also complained that high tariffs, for instance on British steel, benefited industrialists like Carnegie more than his employees who even at the time were regarded by many as being pitifully exploited.

In politics, the two parties engaged in very elaborate get-out-the vote campaigns that succeeded in pushing turnout to 80%, 90%, and even higher. It was financed by the "spoils system" whereby the winning party distributed most local, state and national government jobs, and many government contracts, to its loyal supporters. Large cities were dominated by political machines, in which constituents supported a candidate in exchange for anticipated patronage — favors back from the government, once that candidate was elected — and candidates were selected based on their willingness to play along.

The best known example of a political machine from this time period is Tammany Hall in New York City, led by Boss Tweed. Presidential elections between the two major parties (the Republicans and Democrats), were so closely contested that a slight nudge could tip the teeter-totter to the advantage of the opposition party, and Congress was marked by political stalemate. Mudslinging became an increasingly popular way of gaining advantage at the polls, and Republicans employed an election tactic known as "waving the bloody shirt". Candidates, especially when combating corruption charges, would remind voters that the Republican Party had saved the nation in the Civil War. During the 1870s, voters were repeatedly reminded that the Democrats had been responsible for the bloody upheaval, an appeal that attracted many Union veterans to the Republican camp. The Republicans consistently carried the North in presidential elections.

The South, on the other hand, became the Solid South, nearly always voting Democratic. The political humiliations of Reconstruction were still fresh in many minds. Conversely, the Democrats invoked images of the "lost cause" and the glorious "stars and bars" in much the same way Republicans "waved the bloody shirt." The corruption of the Republican organization led to the defection of a group of reformers called the Mugwumps that supported Democrat Grover Cleveland in 1884. This victory gave Democrats control of the presidency for the first time since the Civil War (not counting the ascension of Andrew Johnson who was technically elected as part of the Union Party).

Overall, Republican and Democratic political platforms remained remarkably constant during the years before 1900. Republicans generally favored inflationary, protectionist policies while Democrats favored hard-money, free trade and other libertarian policies. The negativity and ambiguity of politics began a shift in the press to yellow journalism, in which sensationalism and sentimental stories took as prominent a role as factual news.

Electoral College

From Wikipedia, the free encyclopedia:

The Electoral College is an example of an indirect election, consisting of 538 electors who officially elect the President and Vice President of the United States. The number of electors is equal to the total voting membership of the United States Congress, 435 Representatives and 100 Senators, plus three electors from the District of Columbia.[1] Article II, Section 1, Clause 2 of the Constitution specifies the number of electors to which each state is entitled and state legislatures decide how they are chosen.

Voters in each state and the District of Columbia cast ballots selecting electors pledged to presidential and vice presidential candidates. In nearly all states, electors are awarded on a winner-take-all basis to the candidate who wins the most votes in that state. Although electors are not required by federal law to honor a pledge, in the overwhelming majority of cases they vote for the candidate to whom they are pledged.[2][3] The Twelfth Amendment provides for each elector to cast one vote for President and one vote for Vice President. It also specifies how a President and Vice President are elected. The Twenty-third Amendment specifies how many electors the District of Columbia is entitled to have.

Critics argue that the Electoral College is inherently undemocratic and gives swing states disproportionate influence in electing the President and Vice President. Proponents argue that the Electoral College is an important, distinguishing feature of federalism in the United States and that it protects the rights of smaller states. Numerous constitutional amendments have been introduced in the Congress seeking to alter the Electoral College or replace it with a direct popular vote.

The Electoral College consists of the electors appointed by each state who formally elect the President and Vice President of the United States. Since 1964, there have been 538 electors in each presidential election.[1] Article II, Section 1, Clause 2 of the Constitution specifies how many electors each state is entitled to have and that each state's legislature decides how its electors are to be chosen. U.S. territories are not represented in the Electoral College. The Electoral College is an example of an indirect election, as opposed to a direct election by United

States citizens (such as for members of the United States House of Representatives).

How did the terms "Elector" and "Electoral College" come into usage?

The term "electoral college" does not appear in the Constitution. Article II of the Constitution and the 12th Amendment refer to "electors," but not to the "electoral college." In the Federalist Papers (No. 68), Alexander Hamilton refers to the process of selecting the Executive, and refers to "the people of each State (who) shall choose a number of persons as electors," but he does not use the term "electoral college."

The founders appropriated the concept of electors from the Holy Roman Empire (962 - 1806). An elector was one of a number of princes of the various German states within the Holy Roman Empire who had a right to participate in the election of the German king (who generally was crowned as emperor). The term "college" (from the Latin collegium), refers to a body of persons that act as a unit, as in the college of cardinals who advise the Pope and vote in papal elections. In the early 1800's, the term "electoral college" came into general usage as the unofficial designation for the group of citizens selected to cast votes for President and Vice President. It was first written into Federal law in 1845, and today the term appears in 3 U.S.C. section 4, in the section heading and in the text as "college of electors."

Beware the Tyranny of the Majority

To be brutally honest, the Founding Fathers gave the American public of their day little credit for political awareness when it came to selecting the president. Here are some of their telling statements from the Constitutional Convention of 1787.

> "A popular election in this case is radically vicious. The ignorance of the people would put it in the power of some one set of men dispersed through the Union, and acting in concert, to delude them into any appointment." -- Delegate Gerry, July 25, 1787

> "The extent of the country renders it impossible, that the people can have the requisite capacity to judge of the respective pretensions of the candidates." -- Delegate Mason, July 17, 1787

> "The people are uninformed, and would be misled by a few designing men." -- Delegate Gerry, July 19, 1787

The Founding Fathers had seen the dangers of placing ultimate power into a single set of human hands. Accordingly, they feared that placing unlimited power to elect the president into the politically naive hands of the people could lead to a "tyranny of the majority." In response, they created the Electoral College system as a process to insulate the selection of the president from the whims of the public.

What proposals have been made to change the Electoral College system?

Reference sources indicate that over the past 200 years, over 700 proposals have been introduced in Congress to reform or eliminate the Electoral College. There have been more proposals for Constitutional amendments on changing the Electoral College than on any other subject. The American Bar Association has criticized the Electoral College as "archaic" and "ambiguous" and its polling showed 69 percent of lawyers favored abolishing it in 1987. But surveys of political scientists have supported continuation of the Electoral College. Public opinion polls have shown Americans favored abolishing it by majorities of 58 percent in 1967; 81 percent in 1968; and 75 percent in 1981.

Opinions on the viability of the Electoral College system may be affected by attitudes toward third parties. Third parties have not fared well in the Electoral College system. Candidates with regional appeal such as Governor Thurmond in 1948 and Governor Wallace in 1968 won blocs of electoral votes in the South, which may have affected the outcome, but did not come close to seriously challenging the major party winner. The last third party or splinter party candidate to make a strong showing was Theodore Roosevelt in 1912 (Progressive, also known as the Bull Moose Party). He finished a distant second in electoral and popular votes (taking 88 of the 266 electoral votes needed to win). Although Ross Perot won 19 percent of the popular vote nationwide in 1992, he did not win any electoral votes since he was not particularly strong in any one or several states. Any candidate who wins a majority or plurality of the popular vote has a good chance of winning in the Electoral College, but there are no guarantees (see the results of 1824, 1876, 1888 and 2000 elections)

Our Hidden History of Corporations in the United States

First published February, 2000

When American colonists declared independence from England in 1776, they also freed themselves from control by English corporations that extracted their wealth and dominated trade. After fighting a revolution to end this exploitation, our country's founders retained a healthy fear of corporate power and wisely limited corporations exclusively to a business role. Corporations were forbidden from attempting to influence elections, public policy, and other realms of civic society.

Initially, the privilege of incorporation was granted selectively to enable activities that benefited the public, such as construction of roads or canals. Enabling shareholders to profit was seen as a means to that end.

The states also imposed conditions (some of which remain on the books, though unused) like these:

* Corporate charters (licenses to exist) were granted for a limited time and could be revoked promptly for violating laws.

* Corporations could engage only in activities necessary to fulfill their chartered purpose.

* Corporations could not own stock in other corporations nor own any property that was not essential to fulfilling their chartered purpose.

* Corporations were often terminated if they exceeded their authority or caused public harm.

* Owners and managers were responsible for criminal acts committed on the job.

* Corporations could not make any political or charitable contributions nor spend money to influence law-making.

For 100 years after the American Revolution, legislators maintained tight control of the corporate chartering process. Because of widespread public opposition, early legislators granted very few corporate charters, and only after debate. Citizens governed corporations by detailing operating conditions not just in charters but also in state constitutions and state laws. Incorporated businesses were prohibited from taking any action that legislators did not specifically allow.

States also limited corporate charters to a set number of years. Unless a legislature renewed an expiring charter, the corporation was dissolved and its assets were divided among shareholders. Citizen authority clauses limited capitalization, debts, land holdings, and sometimes, even profits. They required a company's accounting books to be turned over to a legislature upon request. The power of large shareholders was limited by scaled voting, so that large and small investors had equal voting rights. Interlocking directorates were outlawed. Shareholders had the right to remove directors at will.

In Europe, charters protected directors and stockholders from liability for debts and harms caused by their corporations. American legislators explicitly rejected this corporate shield. The penalty for abuse or misuse of the charter was not a plea bargain and a fine, but dissolution of the corporation.

In 1819 the U.S. Supreme Court tried to strip states of this sovereign right by overruling a lower court's decision that allowed New Hampshire to revoke a charter granted to Dartmouth College by King George III. The Court claimed that since the charter contained no revocation clause, it could not be withdrawn. The Supreme Court's attack on state sovereignty outraged citizens. Laws were written or re-written and new state constitutional amendments passed to circumvent the Dartmouth ruling. Over several decades starting in 1844, nineteen states amended their constitutions to make corporate charters subject to alteration or revocation by their legislatures. As late as 1855 it seemed that the Supreme Court had gotten the people's message when in Dodge v. Woolsey it reaffirmed state's powers over "artificial bodies."

But the men running corporations pressed on. Contests over charter were battles to control labor, resources, community rights, and political sovereignty. More and more frequently, corporations were abusing their charters to become conglomerates and trusts. They converted the nation's resources and treasures into private fortunes, creating factory systems and company towns. Political power began flowing to absentee owners, rather than community-rooted enterprises.

The industrial age forced a nation of farmers to become wage earners, and they became fearful of unemployment--a new fear that corporations quickly learned to exploit. Company towns arose. and blacklists of labor organizers and workers who spoke up for their rights became common. When workers began to organize, industrialists and bankers hired private armies to keep them in line. They bought newspapers to paint businessmen as heroes and shape public opinion. Corporations bought state legislators, then announced legislators were corrupt and said that they used too much of the public's resources to scrutinize every charter application and corporate operation.

Government spending during the Civil War brought these corporations fantastic wealth. Corporate executives paid "borers" to infest Congress and state capitals, bribing elected and appointed officials alike. They pried loose an avalanche of government financial largesse. During this time, legislators were persuaded to give corporations limited liability, decreased citizen authority over them, and extended durations of charters. Attempts were made to keep strong charter laws in place, but with the courts applying legal doctrines that made protection of corporations and corporate property the center of constitutional law, citizen sovereignty was undermined. As corporations grew stronger, government and the courts became easier prey. They freely reinterpreted the U.S. Constitution and transformed common law doctrines.

One of the most severe blows to citizen authority arose out of the 1886 Supreme Court case of Santa Clara County v. Southern Pacific Railroad. Though the court did not make a ruling on the question of "corporate personhood," thanks to misleading notes of a clerk, the decision subsequently was used as precedent to hold that a corporation was a "natural person."

From that point on, the 14th Amendment, enacted to protect rights of freed slaves, was used routinely to grant corporations constitutional "personhood." Justices have since struck down hundreds of local, state and federal laws enacted to protect people from corporate harm based on this illegitimate premise. Armed with these "rights," corporations increased control over resources, jobs, commerce, politicians, even judges and the law.

A United States Congressional committee concluded in 1941, "The principal instrument of the concentration of economic power and wealth has been the corporate charter with unlimited power...."

Many U.S.-based corporations are now transnational, but the corrupted charter remains the legal basis for their existence. At ReclaimDemocracy.org, we believe citizens can reassert the convictions of our nation's founders who struggled successfully to free us from corporate rule in the past. These changes must occur at the most fundamental level -- the U.S. Constitution.

Thanks to our friends at the Program on Corporations, Law and Democracy (POCLAD) for their permission to use excerpts of their research for this article.

Please visit our Corporate Personhood page for a huge library of articles exploring this topic more deeply. You might also be interested to read our proposed Constitutional Amendments to revoke illegitimate corporate power, erode the power of money over elections, and establish an affirmative constitutional right to vote.

ReclaimDemocracy.org
Thank you Reclaim Democracy for allowing me to share this with you.

Labor unions in the United States

From Wikipedia, the free encyclopedia

Labor unions are legally recognized as representatives of workers in many industries in the United States. Their activity today centers on collective bargaining over wages, benefits, and working conditions for their membership, and on representing their members in disputes with management over violations of contract provisions. Larger unions also typically engage in lobbying activities and electioneering at the state and federal level.

Most unions in America are aligned with one of two larger umbrella organizations: the AFL-CIO created in 1955, and the Change to Win Federation which split from the AFL-CIO in 2005. Both advocate policies and legislation on behalf of workers in the United States and Canada, and take an active role in politics. The AFL-CIO is especially concerned with global trade issues.

In 2010, the percentage of workers belonging to a union in the United States (or total labor union "density") was 11.4%, compared to 18.6% in Germany, 27.5% in Canada, and 70% in Finland.[1] Union membership in the private sector has fallen under 7%[2] — levels not seen since 1932. Unions allege that employer-incited opposition has contributed to this decline in membership. The most prominent unions are among public sector employees such as teachers and police. Members of unions are disproportionately older, male and residents of the Northeast, the Midwest, and California.[3] Union workers average 10-30% higher pay than non-union in America after controlling for individual, job, and labor market characteristics.[4]

Although much smaller compared to their peak membership in the 1950s, American unions remain a prominent political factor, both through mobilization of their own memberships and through coalitions with like-minded activist organizations around issues such as immigrant rights, trade policy, health care, and living wage campaigns. To fight alleged employer anti-union programs, unions are currently advocating new "card check" federal legislation that would require employers to bargain with a union if more than 50% of workers signed forms, or "cards," stating they wish to be represented by that union. The current procedure involves waiting 45 to 90 days for a federally supervised secret-ballot employee referendum on the subject.

Contents

1 History
   1.1 Post-war
2 Labor unions today
   2.1 Labor negotiations
   2.2 Membership
   2.3 Labor education programs
   2.4 Jurisdiction
3 Possible causes of drop in membership
   3.1 Popularity
   3.2 Recent Polls of Public Opinion and Labor Unions
   3.3 Institutional environments
   3.4 Labor legislation
   3.5 Economic globalization
   3.6 Employer strategies
   3.7 Union responses to globalization
      3.7.1 Transnational labor regulation
4 See also
5 Notes
6 References
   6.1 Surveys
   6.2 To 1900

History

Main article: Labor history of the United States

Unions began forming in the mid-19th century in response to the social and economic impact of the industrial revolution. National labor unions began to form in the post-Civil War Era. The Knights of Labor emerged as a major force in the late 1880s, but it collapsed because of poor organization, lack of effective leadership, and disagreement over goals, and strong opposition from employers and government forces.

The American Federation of Labor, founded in 1886 and led by Samuel Gompers until his death in 1924, proved much more durable. It arose as a loose coalition of various local unions. It helped coordinate and support strikes and eventually became a major player in national politics, usually on the side of the Democrats.

American labor unions benefitted greatly from the New Deal policies of Franklin Delano Roosevelt in the 1930s. The Wagner Act, in particular, legally protected the right of unions to organize. Unions from this point developed increasingly closer ties to the Democratic Party, and are considered a backbone element of the New Deal Coalition. The power and success of labor unions continued to grow after World War II, but faced stiff resistance from conservative, free market business interests, represented politically by the Republican Party.
Post-war

The Taft-Hartley Act of 1947, for example, was a conservative anti-union law that contained numerous measures to weaken unions (for example, by banning union contributions to political candidates and restricting the power of unions to engage in strikes that "threatened national security"). Unions were further weakened in the 1950s by highly publicized reports of corruption in the Teamsters and other unions.

The percentage of workers belonging to a union (or "density") in the United States peaked in 1954 at almost 35% and the total number of union members peaked in 1979 at an estimated 21.0 million. Membership has declined since (currently 14.8 million and 12% of the labor force[2]). Private sector union membership then began a steady decline that continues into the 2010s, but the membership of public sector unions grew steadily (now 37%).[5]

After 1960 public sector unions grew rapidly and secured good wages and high pensions for their members. While manufacturing and farming steadily declined, state- and local-government employment quadrupled from 4 million workers in 1950 to 12 million in 1976 and 16.6 million in 2009.[6] Adding in the 3.7 million federal civilian employees, in 2010 8.4 million government workers were represented by unions,[7] including 31% of federal workers, 35% of state workers and 46% of local workers.[8] As Daniel Disalvo notes, "In today's public sector, good pay, generous benefits, and job security make possible a stable middle-class existence for nearly everyone from janitors to jailors."[9]

Labor unions today

Labor unions in the United States National trade union organization(s)
AFL-CIO, CtW, IWW
National government agency(ies)
United States Department of Labor
National Labor Relations Board
Primary trade union legislation
National Labor Relations Act
Taft-Hartley Act

Trade union membership

16.1 million[10]
Percentage of workforce

- Total: 12.4%
- Public sector: 36.8%
- Private sector: 7.6%

Demographics
- Age 16–24: 5.0%
- 25–34: 10.7%
- 35–44: 13.4%
- 45–54: 16.0%
- 55–64: 16.6%
- 65 and over: 9.0%
- Women: 11.4%
- Men: 13.4%

Standard Occupational Classification

- Management, professional: 13.4%
- Service: 11.9%
- Sales and office: 7.4%
- Natural resources, construction, and maintenance: 17.7%
- Production, transportation, and material moving: 16.4%

International Labour Organization

United States is a member of the ILO
Convention ratification
Freedom of Association   not ratified
Right to Organize   not ratified
Richard Trumka of the AFL-CIO is one of the most prominent union leaders in America

Today most labor unions in the United States are members of one of two larger umbrella organizations: the American Federation of Labor–Congress of Industrial Organizations (AFL-CIO) or the Change to Win Federation, which split from the AFL-CIO in 2005-2006. Both organizations advocate policies and legislation favorable to workers in the United States and Canada, and take an active role in politics favoring the Democratic party but not exclusively so. The AFL-CIO is especially concerned with global trade and economic issues.

Unions have become an issue within the 2008-10 Economic Crisis with the two of the largest automakers receiving $85 billion in loans in order to stay viable. Some conservatives have blamed the near bankruptcy on unions and their 'costly labor agreements' including pension and health plans that put the U.S. automakers at a disadvantage to foreign companies.[11] Others point out that the United Auto Workers has made extensive concessions to the car companies over the last twenty years in order to help the companies remain competitive, and allege that the automakers' recent troubles are better ascribed to other factors.[12][13]

Private sector union members are tightly regulated by the National Labor Relations Act (NLRA), passed in 1935. The law is overseen by the National Labor Relations Board (NLRB), an independent federal agency. Public sector unions are regulated partly by federal and partly by state laws. In general they have shown robust growth rates, for wages and working conditions are set through negotiations with elected local and state officials. The unions' political power thus comes into play, and of course the local government cannot threaten to move elsewhere, nor is there any threat from foreign competition.

To join a traditional labor union, workers must either be given voluntary recognition from their employer or have a majority of workers in a bargaining unit vote for union representation. In either case, the government must then certify the newly formed union. Other forms of unionism include minority unionism, Solidarity unionism, and the practices of organizations such as the Industrial Workers of the World, which do not always follow traditional organizational models.

Public sector worker unions are governed by labor laws and labor boards in each of the 50 states. Northern states typically model their laws and boards after the NLRA and the NLRB. In other states, public workers have no right to establish a union as a legal entity. (About 40% of public employees in the USA do not have the right to organize a legally established union.)
Labor negotiations

Once the union has won the support of a majority of the bargaining unit and is certified in a workplace, it has the sole authority to negotiate the conditions of employment. However, under the NLRA, if a minority of employees voted for a union, those employees can then form a union which represents the rights of only those members who voted for the union. This minority model was once widely used, but was discarded when unions began to consistently win majority support. Unions are beginning to revisit the "members only" model of unionism because of new changes to labor law which unions view as curbing workers' ability to organize.

The employer and the union write the terms and conditions of employment in a legally binding contract. When disputes arise over the contract, most contracts call for the parties to resolve their differences through a grievance process to see if the dispute can be mutually resolved. If the union and the employer still cannot settle the matter, either party can choose to send the dispute to arbitration, where the case is argued before a neutral third party.

Right-to-work statutes forbid unions from negotiating agency shops. Thus, while unions do exist in "right-to-work" states, they are typically weaker.

Members of labor unions enjoy "Weingarten Rights." If management questions the union member on a matter that may lead to discipline or other changes in working conditions, union members can request representation by a union representative. Weingarten Rights are named for the first Supreme Court decision to recognize those rights.[14]

The NLRA goes farther in protecting the right of workers to organize unions. It protects the right of workers to engage in any "concerted activity" for mutual aid or protection. Thus, no union connection is needed. Concerted activity "in its inception involves only a speaker and a listener, for such activity is an indispensable preliminary step to employee self-organization."[15]

Unions are currently advocating new federal legislation, the Employee Free Choice Act (EFCA), that would allow workers to elect union representation by simply signing a support card (card check). The current process established by federal law requires at least 30% of employees to sign cards for the union, then wait 45 to 90 days for a federal official to conduct a secret ballot election in which a simple majority of the employees must vote for the union in order to obligate the employer to bargain.

Unions report that, under the present system, many employers use the 45 to 90 day period to conduct anti-union campaigns. Some opponents of this legislation fear that removing secret balloting from the process will lead to the intimidation and coercion of workers on behalf of the unions. During the 2008 elections, the Employee Free Choice Act had widespread support of many legislators in the House and Senate, and of the President. Since then, support for the "card check" provisions of the EFCA subsided substantially.

Membership
See also: Union affiliation by U.S. state

Union membership had been declining in the US since 1954. In 2007, the labor department reported the first increase in union memberships in 25 years and the largest increase since 1979. Most of the recent gains in union membership have been in the service sector while the number of unionized employees in the manufacturing sector has declined. Most of the gains in the service sector have come in West Coast states like California where union membership is now at 16.7% compared with a national average of about 12.1%.[16] Historically, the rapid growth of public employee unions since the 1960s has served to mask an even more dramatic decline in private-sector union membership.

At the apex of union density in the 1940s, only about 9.8% of public employees were represented by unions, while 33.9% of private, non-agricultural workers had such representation. In this decade, those proportions have essentially reversed, with 36% of public workers being represented by unions while private sector union density had plummeted to around 7%. The US Bureau of Labor Statistics most recent survey indicates that union membership in the US has risen to 12.4% of all workers, from 12.1% in 2007. For a short period, private sector union membership rebounded, increasing from 7.5% in 2007 to 7.6% in 2008.[17] However, that trend has since reversed. In 2009, the union density for private sector stood at 7.2%.[18]

Labor education programs

In the US, labor education programs such as the Harvard Trade Union Program [19] created in 1942 by Harvard University professor John Thomas Dunlop sought to educate union members to deal with important contemporary workplace and labor law issues of the day. The Harvard Trade Union Program is currently part of a broader initiative at Harvard Law School called the Labor and Worklife Program[20] that deals with a wide variety of labor and employment issues from union pension investment funds to the effects of nanotechnology on labor markets and the workplace.

Jurisdiction

Labor unions use the term jurisdiction to refer to their claims to represent workers who perform a certain type of work and the right of their members to perform such work. For example, the work of unloading containerized cargo at United States ports, which the International Longshoremen's Association the International Longshore and Warehouse Union and the International

Brotherhood of Teamsters have claimed rightfully should be assigned to workers they represent. A jurisdictional strike is a concerted refusal to work undertaken by a union to assert its members' right to such job assignments and to protest the assignment of disputed work to members of another union or to unorganized workers. Jurisdictional strikes occur most frequently in the United States in the construction industry.[21]

Unions also use jurisdiction to refer to the geographical boundaries of their operations, as in those cases in which a national or international union allocates the right to represent workers among different local unions based on the place of those workers' employment, either along geographical lines or by adopting the boundaries between political jurisdictions.[21]

Possible causes of drop in membership
Rise and fall of union membership in the United States.

Although most industrialized countries have seen a drop in unionization rates, the drop in union density (the unionized proportion of the working population) has been more significant in the United States than elsewhere. Dropping unionization rates cannot be attributed entirely to changing market structures. In fact, scholars have shown the tremendous complexity inherent in explaining the decline of union density.

Popularity
A historical comparison of union membership as a percentage of all workers and union support in the United States.

Public approval of unions climbed during the 1980s much as it did in other industrialized nations,[22] but declined to below 50% for the first time in 2009 during the Great Recession. It's not clear if this is a long term trend or a function of a high unemployment rate which historically correlates with lower public approval of labor unions.[23]

One explanation for loss of public support is simply the lack of union power or critical mass. No longer do a sizable percentage of American workers belong to unions, or have family members who do. Unions no longer carry the "threat effect": the power of unions to raise wages of non-union shops by virtue of the threat of unions to organize those shops.[23]

Recent Polls of Public Opinion and Labor Unions

A New York Times/CBS Poll found that 60% of Americans opposed restricting collective bargaining while 33% were for it. The poll also found that 56% of Americans opposed reducing pay of public employees compared to 37%. The details of the poll also stated that 26% of those surveyed, thought pay and benefits for public employees were too high, 25% thought too low, and 36% thought about right. Mark Tapscott of the Washington Examiner criticized the poll, accusing it of over-sampling union and public employee households.[24]

A Gallup poll released on March 9 showed that Americans were more likely to support limiting the collective bargaining powers of state employee unions to balance a state's budget (49%) than disapprove of such a measure (45%), while 6% had no opinion. 66% of Republicans approved of such a measure as did 51% of independents. Only 31% of Democrats approved.[25]

A Gallup poll released on March 11 showed that nationwide, Americans were more likely to give unions a negative word or phrase when describing them (38%) than a positive word or phrase (34%). 17% were neutral and 12% didn't know. Republicans were much more likely to say a negative term (58%) than Democrats (19%). Democrats were much more likely to say a positive term (49%) than Republicans (18%).[26]

A nationwide Gallup poll (margin of error ±4%) released on April 1[27] showed the following;

When asked if they supported the labor unions or the governors in state disputes; 48% said they supported the unions, 39% said the governors, 4% said neither, and 9% had no opinion.

Women supported the governors much less than men. 45% of men said they supported the governors, while 46% said they supported the unions. This compares to only 33% of women who said they supported the governors and 50% who said they supported the unions.

All areas of the US (East, Midwest, South, West) were more likely to support unions than the governors. The largest gap being in the East with 35% supporting the governors and 52% supporting the unions, and the smallest gap being in the West with 41% supporting the governors and 44% the unions.

18- to 34-year-olds were much more likely to support unions than those over 34 years of age. Only 27% of 18- to 34-year-olds supported the governors, while 61% supported the unions. Americans ages 35 to 54 slightly supported the unions more than governors, with 40% supporting the governors and 43% the unions. Americans 55 and older were tied when asked, with 45% supporting the governors and 45% the unions.

Republicans were much more likely to support the governors when asked with 65% supporting the governors and 25% the unions. Independents slightly supported unions more, with 40% supporting the governors and 45% the unions. Democrats were overwhelmingly in support of the unions. 70% of Democrats supported the unions, while only 19% supported the governors.

Those who said they were following the situation not too closely or not at all supported the unions over governors, with a 14–point (45% to 31%) margin. Those who said they were following the situation somewhat closely supported the unions over governors by a 52–41 margin. Those who said that they were following the situation very closely were only slightly more likely to support the unions over the governors, with a 49-48 margin.

A nationwide Gallup poll released on August 31 revealed the following:[28]

52% of Americans approved of labor unions, unchanged from 2010.
78% of Democrats approved of labor unions, up from 71% in 2010.
52% of Independents approved of labor unions, up from 49% in 2010.
26% of Republicans approved of labor unions, down from 34% in 2010.

A nationwide Gallup poll released on September 1 revealed the following:[29]

55% of Americans believed that labor unions will become weaker in America as time goes by, an all time high. This compared to 22% who said their power would stay the same, and 20% who said they would get stronger.

The majority of Republicans and Independents believed labor unions would further weaken by a 58% and 57% percentage margin respectively. A plurality of Democrats believed the same, at 46%.

42% of Americans want labor unions to have less influence, tied for the all time high set in 2009. 30% wanted more influence and 25% wanted the same amount of influence.

The majority of Republicans wanted labor unions to have less influence, at 69%.

A plurality of Independents wanted labor unions to have less influence, at 40%.

A plurality of Democrats wanted labor unions to have more influence, at 45%.

The majority of Americans believed labor unions mostly helped members of unions by a 68 to 28 margin.

A plurality of Americans believed labor unions mostly helped the companies where workers are unionized by a 48-44 margin.

A plurality of Americans believed labor unions mostly helped state and local governments by a 47-45 margin.

A plurality of Americans believed labor unions mostly hurt the US economy in general by a 49-45 margin.

The majority of Americans believed labor unions mostly hurt workers who are not members of unions by a 56-34 margin.

Institutional environments

A broad range of forces have been identified as potential contributors to the drop in union density across countries. Sano and Williamson outline quantitative studies that assess the relevance of these factors across countries.[30] The first relevant set of factors relate to the receptiveness of unions' institutional environments. For example, the presence of a Ghent system (where unions are responsible for the distribution of unemployment insurance) and of centralized collective bargaining (organized at a national or industry level as opposed to local or firm level) have both been shown to give unions more bargaining power and to correlate positively to higher rates of union density.[30]

Unions have enjoyed higher rates of success in locations where they have greater access to the workplace as an organizing space (as determined both by law and by employer acceptance), and where they benefit from a corporatist relationship to the state and are thus allowed to participate more directly in the official governance structure. Moreover, the fluctuations of business cycles, particularly the rise and fall of unemployment rates and inflation, are also closely linked to changes in union density.[30]

Labor legislation

Labor lawyer Thomas Geoghegan attributes the drop to the long term effects of the 1947 Taft-Hartley Act, which slowed and then halted labor's growth and then, over many decades, enabled management to roll back its previous gains.[31]

> First, it ended organizing on the grand, 1930s scale. It outlawed mass picketing, secondary strikes of neutral employers, sit downs: in short, everything [Congress of Industrial Organizations founder John L.] Lewis did in the 1930s.

> The second effect of Taft-Hartley was subtler and slower-working. It was to hold up any new organizing at all, even on a quiet, low-key scale. For example, Taft-Hartley ended "card checks." ... Taft-Hartley required hearings, campaign periods, secret-ballot elections, and sometimes more hearings, before a union could be officially recognized.

> It also allowed and even encouraged employers to threaten workers who want to organize. Employers could hold "captive meetings," bring workers into the office and chew them out for thinking about the Union.

And Taft-Hartley led to the "union-busting" that started in the late 1960s and continues today. It started when a new "profession" of labor consultants began to convince employers that they could violate the [pro-labor 1935] Wagner Act, fire workers at will, fire them deliberately for exercising their legal rights, and nothing would happen. The Wagner Act had never had any real sanctions.

[…]

So why hadn't employers been violating the Wagner Act all along? Well, at first, in the 1930s and 1940s, they tried, and they got riots in the streets: mass picketing, secondary strikes, etc. But after Taft-Hartley, unions couldn't retaliate like this, or they would end up with penalty fines and jail sentences.[31]

In general the influence of politics in determining union strength in the US and other countries is contested. Brady[who?] writes that political parties play an expected role in determining union strength, with left-wing governments generally promoting greater union density, other scholars contest this finding by pointing out important counterexamples and explaining the reverse causality inherent in this relationship.[32]

Economic globalization

More recently, as unions have become increasingly concerned with the impacts of market integration on their well-being, scholars have begun to assess whether popular concerns about a global "race to the bottom" are reflected in cross-country comparisons of union strength. These scholars use foreign direct investment (FDI) and the size of a country's international trade as a percentage of its GDP to assess a country's relative degree of market integration. These researchers typically find that globalization does affect union density, but is dependent on other factors, such as unions' access to the workplace and the centralization of bargaining.[33]

Sano and Williamson argue that globalization's impact is conditional upon a country's labor history.[34] In the United States in particular, which has traditionally had relatively low levels of union density, globalization did not appear to significantly affect union density.

Employer strategies

Illegal union firing increased during the Reagan administration and has continued since.[35]

Studies focusing more narrowly on the U.S. labor movement corroborate the comparative findings about the importance of structural factors, but tend to emphasize the effects of changing labor markets due to globalization to a greater extent. Bronfenbrenner notes that changes in the economy, such as increased global competition, capital flight, and the transitions from a manufacturing to a service economy and to a greater reliance on transitory and contingent workers, accounts for only a third of the decline in union density.[36]

Bronfenbrenner claims that the federal government in the 1980s was largely responsible for giving employers the perception that they could engage in aggressive strategies to repress the formation of unions. Richard Freeman also points to the role of repressive employer strategies in reducing unionization, and highlights the way in which a state ideology of anti-unionism tacitly accepted these strategies [22]

Goldfield writes that the overall effects of globalization on unionization in the particular case of the United States may be understated in econometric studies on the subject.[37] He writes that the threat of production shifts reduces unions' bargaining power even if it does not eliminate them, and also claims that most of the effects of globalization on labor's strength are indirect. They are most present in change towards a neoliberal political context that has promoted the deregulation and privatization of some industries and accepted increased employer flexibility in labor markets.

Union responses to globalization

Studies done by Kate Bronfenbrenner at Cornell University show the adverse effects of globalization towards unions due to illegal threats of firing.[38]

Regardless of the actual impact of market integration on union density or on workers themselves, organized labor has been engaged in a variety of strategies to limit the agenda of globalization and to promote labor regulations in an international context. The most prominent example of this has been the opposition of labor groups to free trade initiatives such as the North American Free Trade Agreement (NAFTA) and the Dominican Republic-Central American Free Trade Agreement (DR-CAFTA). In both cases, unions expressed strong opposition to the agreements, but to some extent pushed for the incorporation of basic labor standards in the agreement if one were to pass.[39]

However, Mayer has written that it was precisely unions' opposition to NAFTA overall that jeopardized organized labor's ability to influence the debate on labor standards in a significant way.[40] During Clinton's presidential campaign, labor unions wanted NAFTA to include a side deal to provide for a kind of international social charter, a set of standards that would be enforceable both in domestic courts and through international institutions. Mickey Kantor, then U.S. trade representative, had strong ties to organized labor and believed that he could get unions to come along with the agreement, particularly if they were given a strong voice in the negotiation process.[40]

When it became clear that Mexico would not stand for this kind of an agreement, some critics from the labor movement would not settle for any viable alternatives. In response, part of the labor movement wanted to declare their open opposition to the agreement, and to push for NAFTA's rejection in Congress.[40] Ultimately, the ambivalence of labor groups led those within the Administration who supported NAFTA to believe that strengthening NAFTA's labor side agreement too much would cost more votes among Republicans than it would garner among Democrats, and would make it harder for the United States to elicit support from Mexico.[41]

Graubart writes that, despite unions' open disappointment with the outcome of this labor-side negotiation, labor activists, including the AFL-CIO have used the side agreement's citizen petition process to highlight ongoing political campaigns and struggles in their home countries.[42] He claims that despite the relative weakness of the legal provisions themselves, the side-agreement has served a legitimizing functioning, giving certain social struggles a new kind of standing.

Transnational labor regulation

Unions have recently been engaged in a developing field of transnational labor regulation embodied in corporate codes of conduct. However, O'Brien cautions that unions have been only peripherally involved in this process, and remain ambivalent about its potential effects.[43] They worry that these codes could have legitimizing effects on companies that don't actually live up to good practices, and that companies could use codes to excuse or distract attention from the repression of unions.

Braun and Gearhart note that although unions do participate in the structure of a number of these agreements, their original interest in codes of conduct differed from the interests of human rights and other non-governmental activists. They believed that codes of conduct would be important first steps in creating written principles that a company would be compelled to comply with in later organizing contracts, but did not foresee the establishment of monitoring systems such as the Fair Labor Association. These authors point out that are motivated by power, want to gain insider status politically and are accountable to a constituency that requires them to provide them with direct benefits.

In contrast, activists from the non-governmental sector are motivated by ideals, are free of accountability and gain legitimacy from being political outsiders. Therefore, the interests of unions are not likely to align well with the interests of those who draft and monitor corporate codes of conduct.

Arguing against the idea that high union wages necessarily make manufacturing uncompetitive in a globalized economy is labor lawyer Thomas Geoghegan. Busting

> unions, in the U.S. manner, as the prime way of competing with China and other countries [does not work]. It's no accident that the social democracies, Sweden, France, and Germany, which kept on paying high wages, now have more industry than the U.S. or the UK. ... [T]hat's what the U.S. and the UK did: they smashed the unions, in the belief that they had to compete on cost. The result? They quickly ended up wrecking their industrial base.[44]

Unions have made some attempts to organize across borders. Eder observes that transnational organizing is not a new phenomenon but has been facilitated by technological change.[45] Nevertheless, he claims that while unions pay lip service to global solidarity, they still act largely in their national self-interest. He argues that unions in the global North are becoming increasingly depoliticized while those in the South grow politically, and that global differentiation of production processes leads to divergent strategies and interests in different regions of the world. These structural differences tend to hinder effective global solidarity. However, in light of the weakness of international labor, Herod writes that globalization of production need not be met by a globalization of union strategies in order to be contained.[46]

He points out that local strategies, such as the United Auto Workers' strike against General Motors in 1998, can sometimes effectively interrupt global production processes in ways that they could not before the advent of widespread market integration. Thus, workers need not be connected organizationally to others around the world to effectively influence the behavior of a transnational corporation.

See also

> Labor federation competition in the U.S.
> Union affiliation by U.S. state

History:

> Labor history of the United States
> Timeline of labor unions in the United States
> Commission on Industrial Relations

International:

> Industrial Workers of the World

International comparisons of labor unions

General:

List of strikes
Opposition to trade unions

Notes

^ Trade Union Density OECD. StatExtracts. Retrieved: 17 November 2011.
^ a b Union Members Summary Bureau of Labor Statistics, January 27, 2012 Retrieved: 26 February 2012
^ Not With a Bang, But a Whimper: The Long, Slow Death Spiral of America's Labor Movement| Richard Yeselson| June 6, 2012]
^ 8-31-2004 Union Membership Trends in the United States Gerald Mayer. Congressional Research Service. 8-31-2004
^ Melvyn Dubofsky, and Foster Rhea Dulles, Labor in America: A History (2004)
^ U.S. Census Bureau, "Census Bureau Reports State and Local Government Employment Remains at 16.6 Million" (press release Aug. 10, 2010)
^ This includes some people who are covered by union contracts but are not themselves members.
^ Bureau of Labor Statistics, "Table 3. Union affiliation of employed wage and salary workers by occupation and industry"
^ Daniel Disalvo, "The Trouble with Public Sector Unions", National Affairs" (issue 5 Fall 2010)
^ Bureau of Labor Statistics (January 28, 2009). "Union members in 2008". Washington, D.C.: U.S. Department of Labor.
Greenhouse, Steven (January 28, 2009). "Union membership up sharply in 2008, report says". The New York Times: p. A18.
Whoriskey, Peter (January 29, 2009). "American union ranks grow after 'bottoming out'; first significant increase in 25 years". The Washington Post: p. A8.
^ Cal Thomas: Union to blame for auto industry trouble 15 November 2008
^ Whoriskey, Peter (20 December 2008). "UAW's Sacrifices Look to Some Like Surrender". Washington Post.
^ Maynard, Micheline (2004). The End of Detroit: How the Big Three Lost Their Grip on the American Car Market. Currency/Doubleday. ISBN 0-385-50770-4.
^ NLRB v. J. Weingarten, Inc., 420 U.S. 251 (1975); Tate & Renner Attorneys at Law
^ Root-Carlin, Inc., 92 NLRB 1313, 27 LRRM, 1235, citing NLRB v. City Yellow Cab Co. (6th Cir. 1965), 344 F.2d 575, 582; www.workplacefairness.org

^ Bureau of Labor Statistics (January 25, 2008). "Union members in 2007". Washington, D.C.: U.S. Department of Labor.

Greenhouse, Steven (January 26, 2008). "Union membership sees biggest rise since '83". The New York Times: p. A11.

Freeman, Sholnn (January 26, 2008). "Union membership up slightly in 2007; Growth was biggest in Western states; Midwest rolls shrank with job losses". The Washington Post: p. D2.

^ http://www.bls.gov/news.release/union2.nr0.htm

^ http://www.bls.gov/news.release/union2.t03.htm

^ http://www.law.harvard.edu/programs/lwp/HTUPmission.html

^ http://www.law.harvard.edu/programs/lwp

^ a b Hunt, James W. and Strongin, Patricia K. The Law of the Workplace: Rights of Employers and Employees. 3rd ed. Washington, D.C.: BNA Books, 1994. ISBN 0-87179-841-7; Whitney, Nathaniel Rugges. Jurisdiction in American Building-Trades Unions. Charleston, S.C.: BiblioBazaar, 2008 (originally published 1914). ISBN 0-559-45399-X

^ a b Sexton, Patricia Cayo. "The Decline of the Labor Movement." The Social Movements Reader: Cases and Concepts. Goodwin, Jeff and James M. Jasper, eds. Malden, MA: Blackwell Publishing, 2003

^ a b State Of The Unions by James Surowiecki | newyorker.com | January 17, 2011

^ Tapscott, Mark (March 1, 2011). "CBS News/New York Times survey oversampled union households". Washington Examiner. Retrieved March 2, 2011.

^ "Americans' Message to States: Cut, Don't Tax and Borrow". Gallup.com. 2011-03-09. Archived from the original on 13 March 2011. Retrieved 2011-03-13.

^ "Republicans Negative, Democrats Positive in Describing Unions". Gallup.com. Archived from the original on 14 March 2011. Retrieved 2011-03-12.

^ "More Americans Back Unions Than Governors in State Disputes". Gallup.com. Archived from the original on 6 April 2011. Retrieved 2011-04-03.

^ "Approval of Labor Unions Holds Near Its Low, at 52%". Gallup.com. Retrieved 2011-10-28.

^ "New High of 55% of Americans Foresee Labor Unions Weakening". Gallup.com. Retrieved 2011-10-28.

^ a b c Sano, Joelle and John B. Williamson. (2008) "Factors Affecting Union Decline and their Implications for Labor Reform." International Journal of Comparative Sociology. 49: 479-500

^ a b The United States of Inequality, Entry 6: The Great Divergence and the death of organized labor. By Timothy Noah | slate.com | 12 September 2010

^ Ebbinghaus, B. and Visser, J. (1999) "When Institutions Matter. Union Growth and Decline in Western Europe, 1950–1995", European Sociological Review 15(2): 135–58

^ Scruggs, L. and Lange, P. (2002) 'Where Have all the Members Gone? Globalizations, Institutions, and Union Density', The Journal of Politics 64(1): 126–53.

^ Sano, Joelle and John B. Williamson. (2008) "Factors Affecting Union Decline and their Implications for Labor Reform." International Journal of Comparative Sociology. 49: 479-500.

^ Why America Needs Unions, Business Week

^ Bronfenbrenner, Kate. Organizing to Win: New Research on Union Strategies. Ithaca, N.Y.: ILR Press, 1998

^ Goldfield, Michael. "The impact of globalization and neoliberalism on the decline of organized labor in the United States." Labor, Globalization and the State: Workers, women and migrants confront neoliberalism. Banerjee, Debdas and Michael Goldfield, eds. London: Routledge, 2007.

^ Kate Bronfenbrenner, 'We'll Close', The Multinational Monitor, March 1997, based on the study she directed, 'Final Report: The Effects of Plant Closing or Threat of Plant Closing on the Right of Workers to Organize'.

^ Bolle, Mary Jane. "DR-CAFTA Labor Rights Issues." Congressional Research Service Report for Congress. Order Code RS22159. 8 Jul 2005.

^ a b c Mayer, Frederick. Interpreting NAFTA: The Science and Art of Political Analysis. Columbia International Affairs Online (2006) <http://www.ciaonet.org.libproxy.lib.unc.edu/book/mayer/mayer06.html> (3 Apr 2009)

^ Cameron, Maxwell A. and Brian W. Tomlin. The Making of NAFTA: How the Deal was Done. Ithaca, NY: Cornell University Press, 2000.

^ Graubart, Jonathan. Legalizing Transnational Activism: The Struggle to Gain Social Change from NAFTA's Citizen Petitions. University Park, PA; The Pennsylvania State University Press, 2008.

^ O'Brien, Robert. "The varied paths to minimum global labor standards." Global Unions? Theory and Strategies of organized labor in the global political economy. Harrod, Jeffrey and Robert O'Brien, eds. London: Routledge, 2002.

^ Were You Born On The Wrong Continent? by Thomas Geoghegan

^ Eder, Mine. "The constraints on labor internationalism: contradictions and prospects." Global Unions? Theory and Strategies of organized labor in the global political economy. Harrod, Jeffrey and Robert O'Brien, eds. London: Routledge, 2002.

^ Herod, Andrew. "Organizing globally, organizing locally: union spatial strategy in a global economy." Global Unions? Theory and Strategies of organized labor in the global political economy. Harrod, Jeffrey and Robert O'Brien, eds. London: Routledge, 2002.

References
Surveys

Arnesen, Eric, ed. Encyclopedia of U.S. Labor and Working-Class History (2006), 2064pp; 650 articles by experts excerpt and text search

Beard, Mary Ritter. A Short History of the American Labor Movement 1920 - 176 pages online edition

Beik, Millie, ed. Labor Relations: Major Issues in American History (2005) over 100 annotated primary documents excerpt and text search

Boris, Eileen, and Nelson Lichtenstein, eds. Major Problems In The History Of American Workers: Documents and Essays (2002)

Brody, David. In Labor's Cause: Main Themes on the History of the American Worker (1993) excerpt and text search

Browne, Waldo Ralph. What's what in the Labor Movement: A Dictionary of Labor Affairs and Labor (1921) 577pp; encyclopedia of labor terms, organizations and history. complete text online

Dubofsky, Melvyn, and Foster Rhea Dulles. Labor in America: A History (2004), textbook, based on earlier textbooks by Dulles.

Dubofsky, Melvyn, and Warren Van Tine, eds. Labor Leaders in America (1987) biographies of key leaders, written by scholars excerpt and text search

LeBlanc, Paul. A Short History of the U.S. Working Class: From Colonial Times to the Twenty-First Century (1999), 160pp excerpt and text search

Lichtenstein, Nelson. State of the Union: A Century of American Labor (2003) excerpt and text search

Perlman, Selig. A History of Trade Unionism in the United States 1922 - 313 pages online edition

Taylor, Paul F. The ABC-CLIO Companion to the American Labor Movement (1993) 237pp; short encyclopedia

Zieger, Robert H., and Gilbert J. Gall, American Workers, American Unions: The Twentieth Century(3rd ed. 2002) excerpt and text search

Zieger, Robert H. For Jobs and Freedom: Race and Labor in America Since 1865 (2007) excerpt and text search

To 1900

Commons, John R. History of Labour in the United States - vol 1 and Vol. 2 1860-1896 (1918) vol 2 online edition (note spelling of "Labour")

Commons, John R. "American Shoemakers, 1648-1895: A Sketch of Industrial Evolution," Quarterly Journal of Economics 24 (November, 1909), 39-83. in JSTOR

Commons, John R. ed. Trade Unionism and Labor Problems (1905) articles by experts on unions and working condition online edition

Grob, Gerald N. Workers and Utopia: A Study of Ideological Conflict in the American Labor Movement, 1865-1900 (1961) online edition

Hall, John P. "The Knights of St. Crispin in Massachusetts, 1869-1878," Journal of Economic History 18 (June, 1958), p 161-175 in JSTOR

Laslett, John H. M. Labor and the Left: A Study of Socialist and Radical Influences in the American Labor Movement, 1881-1924 (1970) online edition

Mandel, Bernard. Samuel Gompers: A Biography (1963) online edition

Orth, Samuel P. The Armies of Labor: A Chronicle of the Organized Wage-Earners (1919) short popular overview online edition

Taillon, Paul Michel. Good, Reliable, White Men: Railroad Brotherhoods, 1877-1917 (2009)

Taft, Philip Taft and Philip Ross, "American Labor Violence: Its Causes, Character, and Outcome," in The History of Violence in America: A Report to the National Commission on the Causes and Prevention of Violence, ed. Hugh Davis Graham and Ted Robert Gurr, 1969. online edition

Van Tine, Warren R. The Making of the Labor Bureaucrat: Union Leadership in the United States, 1870-1920 (1973) online edition

Voss, Kim. The Making of American Exceptionalism: The Knights of Labor and Class Formation in the Nineteenth Century (1993) online edition

Weir, Robert E. Beyond Labor's Veil: The Culture of the Knights of Labor (1996) online edition

Bibliography of online resources on railway labor in late 19th century

1900–1932

Bernstein, Irving. The Lean Years: A History of the American Worker, 1920-33 (1966)

Brody, David. Labor in Crisis: The Steel Strike of 1919 (1965)

Dubofsky, Melvyn and Warren Van Tine. John L. Lewis: A Biography (1986)

Brody, David. Labor in Crisis: The Steel Strike of 1919 (1965)

Faue, Elizabeth. Community of Suffering & Struggle: Women, Men, and the Labor Movement in Minneapolis, 1915-1945 (1991)

Fraser, Steve. Labor Will Rule: Sidney Hillman and the Rise of American Labor (1993)

Gordon, Colin. New Deals: Business, Labor, and Politics, 1920-1935 (1994)

Greene, Julie . Pure and Simple Politics: The American Federation of Labor and Political Activism, 1881-1917 (1998)

Hooker, Clarence. Life in the Shadows of the Crystal Palace, 1910-1927: Ford Workers in the Model T Era (1997)

Laslett, John H. M. Labor and the Left: A Study of Socialist and Radical Influences in the American Labor Movement, 1881-1924 (1970)

Karson, Marc. American Labor Unions and Politics, 1900-1918 (1958)

McCartin, Joseph A. 'Labor's Great War: The Struggle for Industrial Democracy and the Origins of Modern American Labor Relations, 1912-1921 (1997)

Mandel, Bernard. Samuel Gompers: A Biography (1963)

Meyer, Stephen. The Five Dollar Day: Labor Management and Social Control in the Ford Motor Company, 1908-1921 (1981)

Mink, Gwendolyn. Old Labor and New Immigrants in American Political Development: Union, Party, and State, 1875-1920 (1986)

Orth, Samuel P. The Armies of Labor: A Chronicle of the Organized Wage-Earners (1919) short overview

Quint, Howard H. The Forging of American Socialism: Origins of the Modern Movement (1964)

Warne, Colston E. ed. The Steel Strike of 1919 (1963), primary and secondary documents

Zieger, Robert. Republicans and Labor, 1919-1929. (1969)

Primary sources

Gompers, Samuel. Seventy Years of Life and Labor: An Autobiography (1925)

1932 - 1955

Bernstein, Irving. Turbulent Years: A History of the American Worker, 1933-1941 (1970)

Boyle, Kevin. The UAW and the Heyday of American Liberalism, 1945-1968 (1995)

Campbell, D'Ann. "Sisterhood versus the Brotherhoods: Women in Unions" Women at War With America: Private Lives in a Patriotic Era (1984).

Dubofsky, Melvyn and Warren Van Time John L. Lewis (1986).

Faue, Elizabeth. Community of Suffering & Struggle: Women, Men, and the Labor Movement in Minneapolis, 1915-1945 (1991), social history

Fraser, Steve. Labor Will Rule: Sidney Hillman and the Rise of American Labor (1993).

Galenson, Walter. The CIO Challenge to the AFL: A History of the American Labor Movement, 1935-1941 (1960)

Gordon, Colin. New Deals: Business, Labor, and Politics, 1920-1935 (1994)

Jensen, Richard J. "The Causes and Cures of Unemployment in the Great Depression," Journal of Interdisciplinary History 19 (1989) p. 553-83

Kennedy, David M. Freedom From Fear: The American People in Depression and War, 1929-1945. (1999) recent narrative.

Lichtenstein, Nelson. Labor's War at Home: The CIO in World War II (2003)

Lichtenstein, Nelson. The Most Dangerous Man in Detroit: Walter Reuther and the Fate of American Labor (1995)

Miller, Sally M., and Daniel A. Cornford eds. American Labor in the Era of World War II (1995), essays by historians, mostly on California

Preis, Art. Labor's Giant Step (1964)

Seidman; Joel. *Brotherhood of Railroad Trainmen: The Internal Political Life of a National Union* (1962)

Vittoz, Stanley. *New Deal Labor Policy and the American Industrial Economy* (1987)

Zieger, Robert H. *The CIO, 1935-1955* (1995)

Fair Employment FEPC

William J. Collins, "Race, Roosevelt, and Wartime Production: Fair Employment in World War II Labor Markets," *American Economic Review* 91:1 (March 2001), pp. 272–286

Andrew Edmund Kersten, *Race, Jobs, and the War: The FEPC in the Midwest, 1941-46* (2000) online review

Merl E. Reed. *Seedtime for the Modern Civil Rights Movement: The President's Committee on Fair Employment Practice, 1941-1946* (1991)

Taft-Hartley and the NLRA

Abraham, Steven E. "The Impact of the Taft-Hartley Act on the Balance of Power in Industrial Relations" *American Business Law Journal* Vol. 33, 1996

Ballam, Deborah A. "The Impact of the National Labor Relations Act on the U.S. Labor Movement" *American Business Law Journal*, Vol. 32, 1995

Brooks, George W., Milton Derber, David A. McCabe, Philip Taft. *Interpreting the Labor Movement* (1952)

Gall, Gilbert J. *The Politics of Right to Work: The Labor Federations as Special Interests, 1943-1979* (1988)

Hartley Jr. Fred A., and Robert A. Taft. *Our New National Labor Policy: The Taft-Hartley Act and the Next Steps* (1948)

Lee, R. Alton. *Truman and Taft-Hartley: A Question of Mandate* (1966)

Millis, Harry A., and Emily Clark Brown. *From the Wagner Act to Taft-Hartley: A Study of National Labor Policy and Labor Relations* (1950)

Primary sources

Christman, Henry M. ed. *Walter P. Reuther: Selected Papers* (1961)

1955–2009

Bennett, James T., and Bruce E. Kaufman. *What do unions do?: a twenty-year perspective* (2007)

Dark; Taylor E. *The Unions and the Democrats: An Enduring Alliance* (1999)

Dine, Philip. *State of the Unions: How Labor Can Strengthen the Middle Class, Improve Our Economy, and Regain Political Influence* (2007)

Fantasia, Rick, and Kim Voss. Hard Work: Remaking the American Labor Movement (2004)

Galenson, Walter; The American Labor Movement, 1955-1995 (1996)

Goldberg, Arthur J. AFL-CIO, Labor United (1956)

Leiter, Robert D. The Teamsters Union: A Study of Its Economic Impact (1957)

Lipset, Seymour Martin, ed. Unions in Transition: Entering the Second Century (1986)

Mort, Jo-Ann, ed. Not Your Father's Union Movement: Inside the AFL-CIO" (2002)

Yates, Michael D. Why Unions Matter (2009)

Fascism

Political scientist Dr. Lawrence Britt recently wrote an article about fascism ("Fascism Anyone?," Free Inquiry, Spring 2003, page 20). Studying the fascist regimes of Hitler (Germany), Mussolini (Italy), Franco (Spain), Suharto (Indonesia), and Pinochet (Chile), Dr. Britt found they all had 14 elements in common. He calls these the identifying characteristics of fascism.
The excerpt is in accordance with the magazine's policy.

14 POINTS OF FASCISM

1. Powerful and continuing expressions of nationalism

From the prominent displays of flags and bunting to the ubiquitous lapel pins, the fervor to show patriotic nationalism, both on the part of the regime itself and of citizens caught up in its frenzy, was always obvious. Catchy slogans, pride in the military, and demands for unity were common themes in expressing this nationalism. It was usually coupled with a suspicion of things foreign that often bordered on xenophobia.

2. Disdain for the importance of human rights

The regimes themselves viewed human rights as of little value and a hindrance to realizing the objectives of the ruling elite. Through clever use of propaganda, the population was brought to accept these human rights abuses by marginalizing, even demonizing, those being targeted. When abuse was egregious, the tactic was to use secrecy, denial, and disinformation.

3. Identification of enemies/scapegoats as a unifying cause

The most significant common thread among these regimes was the use of scapegoating as a means to divert the people's attention from other problems, to shift blame for failures, and to channel frustration in controlled directions. The methods of choice—relentless propaganda and disinformation—were usually effective. Often the regimes would incite "spontaneous" acts against the target scapegoats, usually communists, socialists, liberals, Jews, ethnic and racial minorities, traditional national enemies, members of other religions, secularists, homosexuals, and "terrorists." Active opponents of these regimes were inevitably labeled as terrorists and dealt with accordingly.

4. The supremacy of the military/avid militarism

Ruling elites always identified closely with the military and the industrial infrastructure that supported it. A disproportionate share of national resources was allocated to the military, even when domestic needs were acute. The military was seen as an expression of nationalism, and was used whenever possible to assert national goals, intimidate other nations, and increase the power and prestige of the ruling elite.

5. Rampant sexism

Beyond the simple fact that the political elite and the national culture were male-dominated, these regimes inevitably viewed women as second-class citizens. They were adamantly anti-abortion and also homophobic. These attitudes were usually codified in Draconian laws that enjoyed strong support by the orthodox religion of the country, thus lending the regime cover for its abuses.

6. A controlled mass media

Under some of the regimes, the mass media were under strict direct control and could be relied upon never to stray from the party line. Other regimes exercised more subtle power to ensure media orthodoxy. Methods included the control of licensing and access to resources, economic pressure, appeals to patriotism, and implied threats. The leaders of the mass media were often politically compatible with the power elite. The result was usually success in keeping the general public unaware of the regimes' excesses.

7. Obsession with national security

Inevitably, a national security apparatus was under direct control of the ruling elite. It was usually an instrument of oppression, operating in secret and beyond any constraints. Its actions were justified under the rubric of protecting "national security," and questioning its activities was portrayed as unpatriotic or even treasonous.

8. Religion and ruling elite tied together

Unlike communist regimes, the fascist and proto fascist regimes were never proclaimed as godless by their opponents. In fact, most of the regimes attached themselves to the predominant religion of the country and chose to portray themselves as militant defenders of that religion. The fact that the ruling elite's behavior was incompatible with the precepts of the religion was generally swept under the rug. Propaganda kept up the illusion that the ruling elites were defenders of the faith and opponents of the "godless." A perception was manufactured that opposing the power elite was tantamount to an attack on religion.

9. Power of corporations protected

Although the personal life of ordinary citizens was under strict control, the ability of large corporations to operate in relative freedom was not compromised. The ruling elite saw the corporate structure as a way to not only ensure military production (in developed states), but also as an additional means of social control. Members of the economic elite were often pampered by the political elite to ensure a continued mutuality of interests, especially in the repression of "have-not" citizens.

10. Power of labor suppressed or eliminated

Since organized labor was seen as the one power center that could challenge the political hegemony of the ruling elite and its corporate allies, it was inevitably crushed or made powerless. The poor formed an underclass, viewed with suspicion or outright contempt. Under some regimes, being poor was considered akin to a vice.

11. Disdain and suppression of intellectuals and the arts

Intellectuals and the inherent freedom of ideas and expression associated with them were anathema to these regimes. Intellectual and academic freedom were considered subversive to national security and the patriotic ideal. Universities were tightly controlled; politically unreliable faculty harassed or eliminated. Unorthodox ideas or expressions of dissent were strongly attacked, silenced, or crushed. To these regimes, art and literature should serve the national interest or they had no right to exist.

12. Obsession with crime and punishment

Most of these regimes maintained Draconian systems of criminal justice with huge prison populations. The police were often glorified and had almost unchecked power, leading to rampant abuse. "Normal" and political crime were often merged into trumped-up criminal charges and sometimes used against political opponents of the regime. Fear, and hatred, of criminals or "traitors" was often promoted among the population as an excuse for more police power.

13. Rampant cronyism and corruption

Those in business circles and close to the power elite often used their position to enrich themselves. This corruption worked both ways; the power elite would receive financial gifts and property from the economic elite, who in turn would gain the benefit of government favoritism. Members of the power elite were in a position to obtain vast wealth from other sources as well: for example, by stealing national resources. With the national security apparatus under control and the media muzzled, this corruption was largely unconstrained and not well understood by the general population.

14. Fraudulent elections

Elections in the form of plebiscites or public opinion polls were usually bogus. When actual elections with candidates were held, they would usually be perverted by the power elite to get the desired result. Common methods included maintaining control of the election machinery, intimidating and disenfranchising opposition voters, destroying or disallowing legal votes, and, as a last resort, turning to a judiciary beholden to the power elite.

NOTE: The above 14 Points was written in 2004 by Dr. Laurence Britt, a political scientist. Dr. Britt studied the fascist regimes of: Hitler (Germany), Mussolini (Italy), Franco (Spain), Suharto (Indonesia), and Pinochet (Chile).

Does any of this sound familiar? As America sinks deeper and deeper into corporate greed will this country continue to be a democracy by the people and for the people or will it be ruled by the few? Will the trinity of money, power and greed over come one of the greatest countries in the world? Only we, the people, can keep it free. SPEAK OUT AND LET YOUR THOUGHTS BE KNOWN...ONLY BY SILENCE WILL WE BE DEFEATED!

From Milton Mayer, They Thought They Were Free, The Germans, 1938-45 (Chicago: University of Chicago Press, 1955)

"What no one seemed to notice. . . was the ever widening gap. . .between the government and the people. . . And it became always wider. . . the whole process of its coming into being, was above all diverting, it provided an excuse not to think for people who did not want to think anyway . . . (it) gave us some dreadful, fundamental things to think about . . .and kept us so busy with continuous changes and 'crises' and so fascinated . . . by the machinations of the 'national enemies,' without and within, that we had no time to think about these dreadful things that were growing, little by little, all around us. . .

Each step was so small, so inconsequential, so well explained or, on occasion, 'regretted,' that unless one understood what the whole thing was in principle, what all these 'little measures'. . . must some day lead to, one no more saw it developing from day to day than a farmer in his field sees the corn growing. . . .Each act. . . is worse than the last, but only a little worse. You wait for the next and the next. You wait for one great shocking occasion, thinking that others, when such a shock comes, will join you in resisting somehow.

You don't want to act, or even talk, alone. . . you don't want to 'go out of your way to make trouble.' . . .But the one great shocking occasion, when tens or hundreds or thousands will join with you, never comes. That's the difficulty. The forms are all there, all untouched, all reassuring, the houses, the shops, the jobs, the mealtimes, the visits, the concerts, the cinema, the holidays. But the spirit, which you never noticed because you made the lifelong mistake of identifying it with the forms, is changed. Now you live in a world of hate and fear, and the people who hate and fear do not even know it themselves, when everyone is transformed, no one is transformed. . . .You have accepted things you would not have accepted five years ago, a year ago, things your father. . . could never have imagined." :

As we can see learning about what different political systems do and do not do is important for us to understand what is going on in America, and around the world.
What I am going to do is give you a brief overview of the many types of governments.

Democracy
From Wikipedia, the free encyclopedia

Democracy is a form of government in which all eligible citizens have an equal say in the decisions that affect their lives. Democracy allows people to participate equally—either directly or through elected representatives—in the proposal, development, and creation of laws. It encompasses social, economic and cultural conditions that enable the free and equal practice of political self-determination.

We in America have a version of Democracy that includes fractions of the other forms of government making America unique and I think gives us an edge.

Socialism

From Wikipedia, the free encyclopedia

Socialism is an economic system characterized by social ownership of the means of production and co-operative management of the economy,[1] and a political philosophy advocating such a system. "Social ownership" may refer to cooperative enterprises, common ownership, direct public ownership or autonomous state enterprises.[2] There are many varieties of socialism and there is no single definition encapsulating all of them.[3] They differ in the type of social ownership they advocate, the degree to which they rely on markets or planning, how management is to be organized within productive institutions, and the role of the state in constructing socialism.[4]

I know the Republicans are always going on about Socialism but if we look at the history of this country our democracy is mixed in with socialism.
The schools, roads, parks, police, fire and many other publicly owned utilities are what we call the Commons. The biggest by far Social thing we have is of course the Military and many forget this is Socialism at its purest form.

Fascism

From Wikipedia, the free encyclopedia

Fascism is a radical authoritarian nationalist political ideology.[1][2] Fascists seek to unify their nation based on commitment to an organic national community where its individuals are united together as one people through national identity.[3][4] The unity of the nation is to be based upon suprapersonal connections of ancestry and culture through a totalitarian state that seeks the mass mobilization of the national community through discipline, indoctrination, physical training, and eugenics.[3][4] Fascism utilizes a vanguard party to initiate a revolution to organize the nation upon fascist principles.[5] The fascist party and state is led by a supreme leader who exercises a dictatorship over the party, the government and other state institutions.[6] Fascism views direct action including political violence and war, as a means to achieve national rejuvenation, spirit and vitality.[3][7][8]

Without a doubt we can see fascism cropping up all over America some might call it oligarchy or plutocracy but the bottom line it the rich those like the Koch Brothers would love to end Democracy and set up one the three I just named. Look to States like Michigan, Arizona and Oklahoma and you can see fascism working its ugly head. Like they do with everything the Republicans start things at a lower level and home the skills before taking it national. This is going to be a on going fight until those who vote Republican because the family always had sees that the country is being taken away and freedom will soon follow.

Dictatorship

From Wikipedia, the free encyclopedia

Democracy Index by the Economist Intelligence Unit, 2011.[1] Countries that are more red are authoritarian, and most often dictatorships. Most of current dictatorships are in Africa and Asia.

A dictatorship is defined as an autocratic form of government in which the government is ruled by an individual: a dictator. It has three possible meanings:

A Roman dictator was the incumbent of a political office of legistrate of the Roman Republic. Roman dictators were allocated absolute power during times of emergency. Their power was originally neither arbitrary nor unaccountable, being subject to law and requiring retrospective justification. There were no such dictatorships after the beginning of the 2nd century BC, and later dictators such as Sulla and the Roman Emperors exercised power much more personally and arbitrarily.
A government controlled by one person, or a small group of people. In this form of government the power rests entirely on the person or group of people, and can be obtained by force or by inheritance. The dictator(s) may also take away much of its peoples' freedom.
In contemporary usage, dictatorship refers to an autocratic form of absolute rule by leadership unrestricted by law, constitutions, or other social and political factors within the state.

I know we could never come to this kind of government unless we see a civil war and lets hope we never come to that.

Republic

From Wikipedia, the free encyclopedia

A republic is a form of government in which the country is considered a "public matter" (Latin: res publica), not the private concern or property of the rulers, and where offices of states are subsequently directly or indirectly elected or appointed rather than inherited. In modern times, a common simplified definition of a republic is a government where the head of state is not a monarch.[1][2]

This is one of those that is mixed in with our Democracy.

Oligarchy

From Wikipedia, the free encyclopedia

Oligarchy (from Greek ὀλιγαρχία (oligarkhía); from ὀλίγος (olígos), meaning "a few", and ἄρχω (archo), meaning "to rule or to command")[1][2][3] is a form of power structure in which power effectively rests with a small number of people. These people could be distinguished by royalty, wealth, family ties, education, corporate, or military control. Such states are often controlled by a few prominent families who pass their influence from one generation to the next.[citation needed]

Throughout history, oligarchies have been tyrannical (relying on public servitude to exist) or relatively benign. Aristotle pioneered the use of the term as a synonym for rule by the rich,[4] for which the exact term is plutocracy, but oligarchy is not always a rule by wealth, as oligarchs can simply be a privileged group, and do not have to be connected by bloodlines as in a monarchy. Some[which?] city-states from ancient Greece were oligarchies

Again take a look at my statement about Fascism. There are many on the Right in this country that think this would be a better America and of course they are all from the 1% who care little about America or its history only greed and power.

Theocracy

From Wikipedia, the free encyclopedia

Theocracy is a form of government in which official policy is governed by immediate divine guidance or by officials who are regarded as divinely guided, or is pursuant to the doctrine of a particular religion or religious group.[1][2][3]

Oh yes we have many on the Right that want more of this type of government.

Plutocracy

From Wikipedia, the free encyclopedia

A plutocracy is a government which is ruled by the wealthy, or controlled by wealthy individuals.

The term is usually used pejoratively, as it implies a lack of democratic freedom and social mobility. Numerous historical governments were plutocracies, controlled by an oligarchy composed of the wealthy ruling class, and some modern governments have been accused of being plutocracies, including the United States.

This is in the mix with our current Democracy and we need to keep track of the Plutocrats, this would be those funding the Tea Party and they like most that want to end the current Democracy we have believe in Greed and Power and not in the good of the People.

Communism

From Wikipedia, the free encyclopedia

Communism (from Latin communis - common, universal) is a revolutionary socialist movement to create a classless, moneyless, and stateless social order structured upon common ownership of the means of production, as well as a social, political and economic ideology that aims at the establishment of this social order.[1] This movement, in its Marxist–Leninist interpretations, significantly influenced the history of the 20th century, which saw intense rivalry between the "socialist world" (socialist states ruled by communist parties) and the "western world" (countries with capitalist economies).

Totalitarianism

From Wikipedia, the free encyclopedia

Totalitarianism (or totalitarian rule) is a political system where the state holds total authority over the society and seeks to control all aspects of public and private life wherever necessary.[1]

The concept of totalitarianism was first developed in a positive sense in the 1920's by the Italian fascists. The concept became prominent in Western anti-communist political discourse during the Cold War era in order to highlight perceived similarities between Nazi Germany and other fascist regimes on the one hand, and Soviet communism on the other.[2][3][4][5][6]

Aside from fascist and Stalinist movements, there have been other movements that are totalitarian. The leader of the historic Spanish reactionary conservative movement called the Spanish Confederation of the Autonomous Right declared his intention to "give Spain a true unity, a new spirit, a totalitarian polity..." and went on to say "Democracy is not an end but a means to the conquest of the new state. When the time comes, either parliament submits or we will eliminate it."[7]

Authoritarianism

From Wikipedia, the free encyclopedia

Engelbert Dollfuss's chancellorship in Austria contained many authoritarian elements.

Authoritarianism is a form of social organization characterized by submission to authority as well as the administration of said authority. In politics, an authoritarian government is one in which political authority is concentrated in a small group of politicians.[1] It is usually opposed to individualism and libertarianism.

The Small Business

One of the things that gets me mad is when Republicans talk about the Small Business man. When they really do not care much for the small businessman. They really are talking about Hedge Fund Managers that make millions of dollars but fall under the category of a Small Business.

I have spent the last for years delivering Pizza for a Small Chain that is privately owned. One the things that make this industry so remarkable there are the Mega chains all a way down to the Ma and Pop shops all out there trying to make a living.

Now what you will see from the Republicans, is they want to cut the Min Wage so more jobs can be created. This is really about ending protection for the workers.
For what I can see is that they are dead wrong because just about everyone that can manage at all can have their employees making at least the current min wage and still make profits to stay in business and even expand from a humble beginning.

Republicans like in most things are dead wrong. Statistics show that 97% of all small businesses fall under making over $250,000 a year. Funny those 97% are not supported by the Republicans but the Hedge Fund Managers making millions are the darlings.

Pizza, one of America's greatest businesses

We all love pizza and lets talk about just how amazing this business is.

The Pizza business has its large mega chains some small local chains but it also has many ma and pa pizza parlors to make it a true free market.

The people that run and work there come from all aspects of life, from the young kids starting their first job, to those who maybe lost a job and are searching for their nitch, to those who have made pizza their business for life.

The Pizza Parlor could not be a better place to see just how all facets of business come together. You could say it is manufacturing in motion because all the makings of manufacturing are there. Your bill of material of a pizza is not much different than a bill of material of lets say a Bike.

The order comes in and then all the pieces are gathered and put together and each has its basic parts but there is room to customize.

Got to Love the Pizza Business both in good times and bad it is truly one of god's comfy foods.

"Ideas are like pizza dough, made to be tossed around."
Anna Marie Quindlen (born July 8, 1953) is an American author, journalist, and opinion columnist whose New York Times

"There's no better feeling in the world than a warm pizza box on your lap."
Kevin James (actor), American Actor and Comedian

"You better cut the pizza in four pieces because I'm not hungry enough to eat six."
Yogi Berra, Baseball Player, Coach and just a great character

Ode to the Pizza man:

It all starts with a desire that desire turns into a phone call that call then starts a chain of events.

You give the pizza parlor instructions to that perfect pizza just for your tastes that night.

Handed over to the expertise of what we call the Pie Man, spin your dough high into the air to get the perfect texture before applying those perfect ingredients.

Timer set and into the oven it goes maybe 3 to 7 minutes it is ready and out it comes.

Quickly cut and placed into a pizza box and stuff in a Pizza Bag, now ready to go.

In steps the Pizza Man taking the pizza bag to the car heading out to serve you.

No matter if it is 20 below and snowing or 100 degrees in the shade the Pizza man will deliver.

Some Homes are easy to find some are not but the Pizza Man will always find you.

With a Smile on his face he has delivered that desired Pizza, please always treat your pizza man well.

Jeff Carlson

In order for this country to grow we need to create jobs that allow a person to live. What the Republicans want is to drive wages down so we are at a third world country status and the people live a life of poverty.

The true job creators are not the rich but the everyday person out there spending the money they make. In order to do this correctly an individual must be making a living wage and spending it on the day to day things we need to function in the America we have evolved into. This is truly what that makes the economy hum. This is demand side economics and exactly what the Republicans oppose because they know it works well for the middle class.

They believe in giving tax breaks and money to the rich along with deregulation of consumer protection laws. We tried this under the Bush Admin and he destroyed the economy and we came close to a major depression.
The other time Austerity was used caused the Gilded Age Depression and the Great Depression back in the 20's 30's.

This battle will be ongoing with Right Wing Ideology firmly in place in this country.

MOVING FORWARD

"This November will go down in History as one of those times where this country had a chance to right itself. Or will be ended by Right Wing Ideology setting a path of destruction and the ending of Democracy."
Jeff Carlson

Abraham Lincoln, warned us many years ago and we sit now in crossroads and this election will determine the fate of America from this day forward. Do we continue as a Democracy or do we fall to a Fascist Right Wing World that be the death of our country.

Speech by Abraham Lincoln,
Speech given at the Young Men's Lyceum of Springfield, Illinois January 27, 1838

As a subject for the remarks of the evening, "The perpetuation of our political institutions" is selected.

In the great journal of things happening under the sun, we, the American people, find our account running under date of the nineteenth century of the Christian era. We find ourselves in the peaceful possession of the fairest portion of the earth as regards extent of territory, fertility of soil, and salubrity of climate. We find ourselves under the government of a system of political institutions conducing more essentially to the ends of civil and religious liberty than any of which the history of former times tells us. We, when mounting the stage of existence, found ourselves the legal inheritors of these fundamental blessings. We toiled not in the acquirement or establishment of them; they are a legacy bequeathed us by a once hardy, brave, and patriotic, but now lamented and departed, race of ancestors. Theirs was the task (and nobly they performed it) to possess themselves, and through themselves us, of this goodly land, and to uprear upon its hills and its valleys a political edifice of liberty and equal rights; 'tis ours only to transmit these — the former unprofaned by the foot of an invader, the latter undecayed by the lapse of time and untorn by usurpation — to the latest generation that fate shall permit the world to know. This task of gratitude to our fathers, justice to ourselves, duty to posterity, and love for our species in general, all imperatively require us faithfully to perform.

How then shall we perform it? At what point shall we expect the approach of danger? By what means shall we fortify against it? Shall we expect some transatlantic military giant to step the ocean and crush us at a blow? Never! **All the armies of Europe, Asia, and Africa combined, with all the treasure of the**

earth (our own excepted) in their military chest, with a Bonaparte for a commander, could not by force take a drink from the Ohio or make a track on the Blue Ridge in a trial of a thousand years.

At what point, then, is the approach of danger to be expected? I answer, If it ever reach us it must spring up amongst us; it cannot come from abroad. If destruction be our lot we must ourselves be its author and finisher. As a nation of freemen we must live through all time, or die by suicide.

What Abe said, "**As a nation of freemen we must live through all time, or die by suicide.**" This is where I see America at this point and we need to make sure we do not fail to vote to save this country from a right wing ideology that is bent on turning us into a third world country.

The Democratic Convention was the first time I think the democrats have grown a backbone and one by one the speakers called out the Lies and Misinformation of the Republicans.

Here is some selected quotes from the Speech from former President Bill Clinton. He was specific and went over all the aspects of the lies now being aired all over the country on TV.

The Republicans are so use to lying they never expected anyone to call them on it.

This book is dedicated to this election and the paths that we can take and I could not say it any better than these two wonderful brilliant men did in their speeches, Bill Clinton and Barrack Obama, did in their speeches at the Convention. Here they are and what they say must be known because we may never get a chance again to do it right.

Text of former President Bill Clinton as delivered at the Democratic National Convention

We're here to nominate a President, and I've got one in mind.

I want to nominate a man whose own life has known its fair share of adversity and uncertainty. A man who ran for President to change the course of an already weak economy and then just six weeks before the election, saw it suffer the biggest collapse since the Great Depression. A man who stopped the slide into depression and put us on the long road to recovery, knowing all the while that no matter how many jobs were created and saved, there were still millions more waiting, trying to feed their children and keep their hopes alive.

I want to nominate a man cool on the outside but burning for America on the inside. A man who believes we can build a new American Dream economy driven by innovation and creativity, education and cooperation. A man who had the good sense to marry Michelle Obama.

I want Barack Obama to be the next President of the United States and I proudly nominate him as the standard bearer of the Democratic Party.

In Tampa, we heard a lot of talk about how the President and the Democrats don't believe in free enterprise and individual initiative, how we want everyone to be dependent on the government, how bad we are for the economy.

The Republican narrative is that all of us who amount to anything are completely self-made. One of our greatest Democratic Chairmen, Bob Strauss, used to say that every politician wants you to believe he was born in a log cabin he built himself, but it ain't so.

We Democrats think the country works better with a strong middle class, real opportunities for poor people to work their way into it and a relentless focus on the future, with business and government working together to promote growth and broadly shared prosperity. We think "we're all in this together" is a better philosophy than "you're on your own."

Who's right? Well since 1961, the Republicans have held the White House 28 years, the Democrats 24. In those 52 years, our economy produced 66 million private sector jobs. What's the jobs score? Republicans 24 million, Democrats 42 million!

It turns out that advancing equal opportunity and economic empowerment is both morally right and good economics, because discrimination, poverty and ignorance restrict growth, while investments in education, infrastructure and scientific and technological research increase it, creating more good jobs and new wealth for all of us.

Though I often disagree with Republicans, I never learned to hate them the way the far right that now controls their party seems to hate President Obama and the Democrats. After all, President Eisenhower sent federal troops to my home state to integrate Little Rock Central High and built the interstate highway system. And as governor, I worked with President Reagan on welfare reform and with President George H.W. Bush on national education goals. I am grateful to President George W. Bush for PEPFAR, which is saving the lives of millions of people in poor countries and to both Presidents Bush for the work we've done together after the South Asia tsunami, Hurricane Katrina and the Haitian earthquake.

Through my foundation, in America and around the world, I work with Democrats, Republicans and Independents who are focused on solving problems and seizing opportunities, not fighting each other.

When times are tough, constant conflict may be good politics but in the real world, cooperation works better. After all, nobody's right all the time, and a broken clock is right twice a day. All of us are destined to live our lives between those two extremes. Unfortunately, the faction that now dominates the Republican Party doesn't see it that way. They think government is the enemy, and compromise is weakness.

One of the main reasons America should re-elect President Obama is that he is still committed to cooperation. He appointed Republican Secretaries of Defense, the Army and Transportation. He appointed a Vice President who ran against him in 2008, and trusted him to oversee the successful end of the war in Iraq and the implementation of the recovery act. And Joe Biden did a great job with both. He appointed Cabinet members who supported Hillary in the primaries. Heck, he even appointed Hillary! I'm so proud of her and grateful to our entire national security team for all they've done to make us safer and stronger and to build a world with more partners and fewer enemies. I'm also grateful to the young men and women who serve our country in the military and to Michelle Obama and Jill Biden for supporting military families when their loved ones are overseas and for helping our veterans, when they come home bearing the wounds of war, or needing help with education, housing, and jobs.

President Obama's record on national security is a tribute to his strength, and judgment, and to his preference for inclusion and partnership over partisanship.

He also tried to work with Congressional Republicans on Health Care, debt reduction, and jobs, but that didn't work out so well. Probably because, as the Senate Republican leader, in a remarkable moment of candor, said two years before the election, their number one priority was not to put America back to work, but to put President Obama out of work.

Senator, I hate to break it to you, but we're going to keep President Obama on the job!

In Tampa, the Republican argument against the President's re-election was pretty simple: we left him a total mess, he hasn't cleaned it up fast enough, so fire him and put us back in.

In order to look like an acceptable alternative to President Obama, they couldn't say much about the ideas they have offered over the last two years. You see they want to go back to the same old policies that got us into trouble in the first place: to cut taxes for high income Americans even more than President Bush did; to get rid of those pesky financial regulations designed to prevent another crash and prohibit future bailouts; to increase defense spending two trillion dollars more than the Pentagon has requested without saying what they'll spend the money on; to make enormous cuts in the rest of the budget, especially programs that help the middle class and poor kids. As another President once said – there they go again.

I like the argument for President Obama's re-election a lot better. He inherited a deeply damaged economy, put a floor under the crash, began the long hard road to recovery, and laid the foundation for a modern, more well-balanced economy that will produce millions of good new jobs, vibrant new businesses, and lots of new wealth for the innovators.

Are we where we want to be? No. Is the President satisfied? No. Are we better off than we were when he took office, with an economy in free fall, losing 750,000 jobs a month. The answer is YES.

I understand the challenge we face. I know many Americans are still angry and frustrated with the economy. Though employment is growing, banks are beginning to lend and even housing prices are picking up a bit, too many people don't feel it.

I experienced the same thing in 1994 and early 1995. Our policies were working and the economy was growing but most people didn't feel it yet. By 1996, the economy was roaring, halfway through the longest peacetime expansion in American history.

President Obama started with a much weaker economy than I did. No President – not me or any of my predecessors could have repaired all the damage in just four years. But conditions are improving and if you'll renew the President's contract you will feel it.

I believe that with all my heart.

President Obama's approach embodies the values, the ideas, and the direction America must take to build a 21st century version of the American Dream in a nation of shared opportunities, shared prosperity and shared responsibilities.

So back to the story. In 2010, as the President's recovery program kicked in, the job losses stopped and things began to turn around.

The Recovery Act saved and created millions of jobs and cut taxes for 95% of the American people. In the last 29 months the economy has produced about 4.5 million private sector jobs. But last year, the Republicans blocked the President's jobs plan costing the economy more than a million new jobs. So here's another jobs score: President Obama plus 4.5 million, Congressional Republicans zero.

Over that same period, more than more than 500,000 manufacturing jobs have been created under President Obama – the first time manufacturing jobs have increased since the 1990s.

The auto industry restructuring worked. It saved more than a million jobs, not just at GM, Chrysler and their dealerships, but in auto parts manufacturing all over the country. That's why even auto-makers that weren't part of the deal supported it. They needed to save the suppliers too. Like I said, we're all in this together.

Now there are 250,000 more people working in the auto industry than the day the companies were restructured. Governor Romney opposed the plan to save GM and Chrysler. So here's another jobs score: Obama two hundred and fifty thousand, Romney, zero.

The agreement the administration made with management, labor and environmental groups to double car mileage over the next few years is another good deal: it will cut your gas bill in half, make us more energy independent, cut greenhouse gas emissions, and add another 500,000 good jobs.

President Obama's "all of the above" energy plan is helping too – the boom in oil and gas production combined with greater energy efficiency has driven oil imports to a near 20 year low and natural gas production to an all time high. Renewable energy production has also doubled.

We do need more new jobs, lots of them, but there are already more than three million jobs open and unfilled in America today, mostly because the applicants don't have the required skills. We have to prepare more Americans for the new jobs that are being created in a world fueled by new technology. That's why investments in our people are more important than ever. The President has supported community colleges and employers in working together to train people for open jobs in their communities. And, after a decade in which exploding college costs have increased the drop-out rate so much that we've fallen to 16th in the world in the percentage of our young adults with college degrees, his student loan reform lowers the cost of federal student loans and even more important, gives students the right to repay the loans as a fixed percentage of their incomes for up to 20 years. That means no one will have to drop-out of college for fear they can't repay their debt, and no one will have to turn down a job, as a teacher, a police officer or a small town doctor because it doesn't pay enough to make the debt payments. This will change the future for young Americans.

I know we're better off because President Obama made these decisions.

That brings me to health care.

The Republicans call it Obamacare and say it's a government takeover of health care that they'll repeal. Are they right? Let's look at what's happened so far. Individuals and businesses have secured more than a billion dollars in refunds from their insurance premiums because the new law requires 80% to 85% of your premiums to be spent on health care, not profits or promotion. Other insurance companies have lowered their rates to meet the requirement. More than 3 million young people between 19 and 25 are insured for the first time because their parents can now carry them on family policies. Millions of seniors are receiving preventive care including breast cancer screenings and tests for heart problems. Soon the insurance companies, not the government, will have millions of new customers many of them middle class people with pre-existing conditions. And for the last two years, health care spending has grown under 4%, for the first time in 50 years.

So are we all better off because President Obama fought for it and passed it? You bet we are.

There were two other attacks on the President in Tampa that deserve an answer. Both Governor Romney and Congressman Ryan attacked the President for allegedly robbing Medicare of 716 billion dollars. Here's what really happened. There were no cuts to benefits. None. What the President did was save money by cutting unwarranted subsidies to providers and insurance companies that weren't making people any healthier. He used the saving to close the donut hole in the Medicare drug program, and to add eight years to the life of the Medicare Trust Fund. It's now solvent until 2024. So President Obama and the Democrats didn't weaken Medicare, they strengthened it.

When Congressman Ryan looked into the TV camera and attacked President Obama's "biggest coldest power play" in raiding Medicare, I didn't know whether to laugh or cry. You see, that 716 billion dollars is exactly the same amount of Medicare savings Congressman Ryan had in his own budget.

At least on this one, Governor Romney's been consistent. He wants to repeal the savings and give the money back to the insurance companies, re-open the donut hole and force seniors to pay more for drugs, and reduce the life of the Medicare Trust Fund by eight years. So now if he's elected and does what he promised Medicare will go broke by 2016. If that happens, you won't have to wait until their voucher program to begins in 2023 to see the end Medicare as we know it.

But it gets worse. They also want to block grant Medicaid and cut it by a third over the coming decade. Of course, that will hurt poor kids, but that's not all. Almost two-thirds of Medicaid is spent on nursing home care for seniors and on people with disabilities, including kids from middle class families, with special needs like, Downs syndrome or Autism. I don't know how those families are going to deal with it. We can't let it happen

Now let's look at the Republican charge that President Obama wants to weaken the work requirements in the welfare reform bill I signed that moved millions of people from welfare to work.

Here's what happened. When some Republican governors asked to try new ways to put people on welfare back to work, the Obama Administration said they would only do it if they had a credible plan to increase employment by 20%. You hear that? More work. So the claim that President Obama weakened welfare reform's work requirement is just not true. But they keep running ads on it. As their campaign pollster said "we're not going to let our campaign be dictated by fact checkers." Now that is true. I couldn't have said it better myself – I just hope you remember that every time you see the ad.

Let's talk about the debt. We have to deal with it or it will deal with us. President Obama has offered a plan with 4 trillion dollars in debt reduction over a decade, with two and a half dollars of spending reductions for every one dollar of revenue increases, and tight controls on future spending. It's the kind of balanced approach proposed by the bipartisan Simpson-Bowles commission.

I think the President's plan is better than the Romney plan, because the Romney plan fails the first test of fiscal responsibility: The numbers don't add up.

It's supposed to be a debt reduction plan but it begins with five trillion dollars in tax cuts over a ten-year period. That makes the debt hole bigger before they even start to dig out. They say they'll make it up by eliminating loopholes in the tax code. When you ask "which loopholes and how much?," they say "See me after the election on that."

People ask me all the time how we delivered four surplus budgets. What new ideas did we bring? I always give a one-word answer: arithmetic. If they stay with a 5 trillion dollar tax cut in a debt reduction plan – the – arithmetic tells us that one of three things will happen: 1) they'll have to eliminate so many deductions like the ones for home mortgages and charitable giving that middle class families will see their tax bill go up two thousand dollars year while people making over 3 million dollars a year get will still get a 250,000 dollar tax cut; or 2) they'll have to cut so much spending that they'll obliterate the budget for our national parks, for ensuring clean air, clean water, safe food, safe air travel; or they'll cut way back on Pell Grants, college loans, early childhood education and other programs that help middle class families and poor children, not to mention cutting investments in roads, bridges, science, technology and medical research; or 3) they'll do what they've been doing for thirty plus years now – cut taxes more than they cut spending, explode the debt, and weaken the economy. Remember, Republican economic policies quadrupled the debt before I took office and doubled it after I left. We simply can't afford to double-down on trickle-down.

President Obama's plan cuts the debt, honors our values, and brightens the future for our children, our families and our nation.

My fellow Americans, you have to decide what kind of country you want to live in. If you want a you're on your own, winner take all society you should support the Republican ticket. If you want a country of shared opportunities and shared responsibilities – a "we're all in it together" society, you should vote for Barack Obama and Joe Biden. If you want every American to vote and you think its wrong to change voting procedures just to reduce the turnout of younger, poorer, minority and disabled voters, you should support Barack Obama. If you think the President was right to open the doors of American opportunity to young immigrants brought here as children who want to go to college or serve in the military, you should vote for Barack Obama. If you want a future of shared prosperity, where the middle class is growing and poverty is declining, where the American Dream is alive and well, and where the United States remains the leading force for peace and prosperity in a highly competitive world, you should vote for Barack Obama.

I love our country – and I know we're coming back. For more than 200 years, through every crisis, we've always come out stronger than we went in. And we will again as long as we do it together. We champion the cause for which our founders pledged their lives, their fortunes, and their sacred honor – to form a more perfect union.

If that's what you believe, if that's what you want, we have to re-elect President Barack Obama.

God Bless You – God Bless America.

There are so many great points in this speech but what I want to point out is the two big LIES that Clinton did such a masterful job of calling them out.

The first one was about the 716 million in Medicare Savings that the Republicans are running ads saying Obama Stole the Money for Obamacare with the people losing. Total Lie.

The second was where he talks about the Welfare System he signed into place and how Obama change the rules so no work required. Another bone face LIE.

Text of President Barack Obama's remarks Thursday night at the Democratic National Convention, as provided by the Obama campaign:

Michelle, I love you. The other night, I think the entire country saw just how lucky I am. Malia and Sasha, you make me so proud . but don't get any ideas, you're still going to class tomorrow. And Joe Biden, thank you for being the best vice president I could ever hope for.

Madam Chairwoman, delegates, I accept your nomination for president of the United States.

The first time I addressed this convention in 2004, I was a younger man; a senate candidate from Illinois who spoke about hope_ not blind optimism or wishful thinking, but hope in the face of difficulty; hope in the face of uncertainty; that dogged faith in the future which has pushed this nation forward, even when the odds are great; even when the road is long.

Eight years later, that hope has been tested_ by the cost of war; by one of the worst economic crises in history; and by political gridlock that's left us wondering whether it's still possible to tackle the challenges of our time.

I know that campaigns can seem small, and even silly. Trivial things become big distractions. Serious issues become sound bites. And the truth gets buried under an avalanche of money and advertising. If you're sick of hearing me approve this message, believe me_ so am I.

But when all is said and done_ when you pick up that ballot to vote_ you will face the clearest choice of any time in a generation. Over the next few years, big decisions will be made in Washington, on jobs and the economy; taxes and deficits; energy and education; war and peace_ decisions that will have a huge impact on our lives and our children's lives for decades to come.

On every issue, the choice you face won't be just between two candidates or two parties.

It will be a choice between two different paths for America.

A choice between two fundamentally different visions for the future.

Ours is a fight to restore the values that built the largest middle class and the strongest economy the world has ever known; the values my grandfather defended as a soldier in Patton's Army; the values that drove my grandmother to work on a bomber assembly line while he was gone.

They knew they were part of something larger_ a nation that triumphed over fascism and depression; a nation where the most innovative businesses turned out the world's best products, and everyone shared in the pride and success_ from the corner office to the factory floor. My grandparents were given the chance to go to college, buy their first home, and fulfill the basic bargain at the heart of America's story: the promise that hard work will pay off; that responsibility will be rewarded; that everyone gets a fair shot, and everyone does their fair share, and everyone plays by the same rules_ from Main Street to Wall Street to Washington, D.C.

I ran for president because I saw that basic bargain slipping away. I began my career helping people in the shadow of a shuttered steel mill, at a time when too many good jobs were starting to move overseas. And by 2008, we had seen nearly a decade in which families struggled with costs that kept rising but paychecks that didn't; racking up more and more debt just to make the mortgage or pay tuition; to put gas in the car or food on the table. And when the house of cards collapsed in the Great Recession, millions of innocent Americans lost their jobs, their homes, and their life savings_ a tragedy from which we are still fighting to recover.

Now, our friends at the Republican convention were more than happy to talk about everything they think is wrong with America, but they didn't have much to say about how they'd make it right. They want your vote, but they don't want you to know their plan. And that's because all they have to offer is the same prescription they've had for the last thirty years:

"Have a surplus? Try a tax cut."

"Deficit too high? Try another."

"Feel a cold coming on? Take two tax cuts, roll back some regulations, and call us in the morning!"

Now, I've cut taxes for those who need it_ middle-class families and small businesses. But I don't believe that another round of tax breaks for millionaires will bring good jobs to our shores, or pay down our deficit. I don't believe that firing teachers or kicking students off financial aid will grow the economy, or help us compete with the scientists and engineers coming out of China. After all that we've been through, I don't believe that rolling back regulations on Wall Street will help the small businesswoman expand, or the laid-off construction worker keep his home. We've been there, we've tried that, and we're not going back. We're moving forward.

I won't pretend the path I'm offering is quick or easy. I never have. You didn't elect me to tell you what you wanted to hear. You elected me to tell you the truth. And the truth is, it will take more than a few years for us to solve challenges that have built up over decades. It will require common effort, shared responsibility, and the kind of bold, persistent experimentation that Franklin Roosevelt pursued during the only crisis worse than this one. And by the way_ those of us who carry on his party's legacy should remember that not every problem can be remedied with another government program or dictate from Washington.

But know this, America: Our problems can be solved. Our challenges can be met. The path we offer may be harder, but it leads to a better place. And I'm asking you to choose that future. I'm asking you to rally around a set of goals for your country_ goals in manufacturing, energy, education, national security, and the deficit; a real, achievable plan that will lead to new jobs, more opportunity, and rebuild this economy on a stronger foundation. That's what we can do in the next four years, and that's why I'm running for a second term as president of the United States.

We can choose a future where we export more products and outsource fewer jobs. After a decade that was defined by what we bought and borrowed, we're getting back to basics, and doing what America has always done best:

We're making things again.

I've met workers in Detroit and Toledo who feared they'd never build another American car. Today, they can't build them fast enough, because we reinvented a dying auto industry that's back on top of the world.

I've worked with business leaders who are bringing jobs back to America_ not because our workers make less pay, but because we make better products. Because we work harder and smarter than anyone else.

I've signed trade agreements that are helping our companies sell more goods to millions of new customers_ goods that are stamped with three proud words: Made in America.

After a decade of decline, this country created over half a million manufacturing jobs in the last two and a half years. And now you have a choice: we can give more tax breaks to corporations that ship jobs overseas, or we can start rewarding companies that open new plants and train new workers and create new jobs here, in the United States of America. We can help big factories and small businesses double their exports, and if we choose this path, we can create a million new manufacturing jobs in the next four years. You can make that happen. You can choose that future.

You can choose the path where we control more of our own energy. After 30 years of inaction, we raised fuel standards so that by the middle of the next decade, cars and trucks will go twice as far on a gallon of gas. We've doubled our use of renewable energy, and thousands of Americans have jobs today building wind turbines and long-lasting batteries. In the last year alone, we cut oil imports by 1 million barrels a day_ more than any administration in recent history. And today, the United States of America is less dependent on foreign oil than at any time in nearly two decades.

Now you have a choice_ between a strategy that reverses this progress, or one that builds on it. We've opened millions of new acres for oil and gas exploration in the last three years, and we'll open more. But unlike my opponent, I will not let oil companies write this country's energy plan, or endanger our coastlines, or collect another $4 billion in corporate welfare from our taxpayers.

We're offering a better path a future where we keep investing in wind and solar and clean coal; where farmers and scientists harness new biofuels to power our cars and trucks; where construction workers build homes and factories that waste less energy; where we develop a hundred year supply of natural gas that's right beneath our feet. If you choose this path, we can cut our oil imports in half by 2020 and support more than 600,000 new jobs in natural gas alone.

And yes, my plan will continue to reduce the carbon pollution that is heating our planet_ because climate change is not a hoax. More droughts and floods and wildfires are not a joke. They're a threat to our children's future. And in this election, you can do something about it.

You can choose a future where more Americans have the chance to gain the skills they need to compete, no matter how old they are or how much money they have. Education was the gateway to opportunity for me. It was the gateway for Michelle. And now more than ever, it is the gateway to a middle-class life.

For the first time in a generation, nearly every state has answered our call to raise their standards for teaching and learning. Some of the worst schools in the country have made real gains in math and reading. Millions of students are paying less for college today because we finally took on a system that wasted billions of taxpayer dollars on banks and lenders.

And now you have a choice_ we can gut education, or we can decide that in the United States of America, no child should have her dreams deferred because of a crowded classroom or a crumbling school. No family should have to set aside a college acceptance letter because they don't have the money. No company should have to look for workers in China because they couldn't find any with the right skills here at home.

Government has a role in this. But teachers must inspire; principals must lead; parents must instill a thirst for learning, and students, you've got to do the work. And together, I promise you_ we can out-educate and out-compete any country on Earth. Help me recruit 100,000 math and science teachers in the next ten years, and improve early childhood education. Help give 2 million workers the chance to learn skills at their community college that will lead directly to a job. Help us work with colleges and universities to cut in half the growth of tuition costs over the next 10 years. We can meet that goal together. You can choose that future for America.

In a world of new threats and new challenges, you can choose leadership that has been tested and proven. Four years ago, I promised to end the war in Iraq. We did. I promised to refocus on the terrorists who actually attacked us on 9/11. We have. We've blunted the Taliban's momentum in Afghanistan, and in 2014, our longest war will be over. A new tower rises above the New York skyline, al-Qaida is on the path to defeat, and Osama bin Laden is dead.

Tonight, we pay tribute to the Americans who still serve in harm's way. We are forever in debt to a generation whose sacrifice has made this country safer and more respected. We will never forget you. And so long as I'm commander in chief, we will sustain the strongest military the world has ever known. When you take off the uniform, we will serve you as well as you've served us_ because no one who fights for this country should have to fight for a job, or a roof over their head, or the care that they need when they come home.

Around the world, we've strengthened old alliances and forged new coalitions to stop the spread of nuclear weapons. We've reasserted our power across the Pacific and stood up to China on behalf of our workers. From Burma to Libya to South Sudan, we have advanced the rights and dignity of all human beings_ men and women; Christians and Muslims and Jews.

But for all the progress we've made, challenges remain. Terrorist plots must be disrupted. Europe's crisis must be contained. Our commitment to Israel's security must not waver, and neither must our pursuit of peace. The Iranian government must face a world that stays united against its nuclear ambitions. The historic change sweeping across the Arab World must be defined not by the iron fist of a dictator or the hate of extremists, but by the hopes and aspirations of ordinary people who are reaching for the same rights that we celebrate today.

So now we face a choice. My opponent and his running mate are new to foreign policy, but from all that we've seen and heard, they want to take us back to an era of blustering and blundering that cost America so dearly.

After all, you don't call Russia our number one enemy_ and not al-Qaida_ unless you're still stuck in a Cold War time warp. You might not be ready for diplomacy with Beijing if you can't visit the Olympics without insulting our closest ally. My opponent said it was "tragic" to end the war in Iraq, and he won't tell us how he'll end the war in Afghanistan. I have, and I will. And while my opponent would spend more money on military hardware that our joint chiefs don't even want, I'll use the money we're no longer spending on war to pay down our debt and put more people back to work_ rebuilding roads and bridges; schools and runways. After two wars that have cost us thousands of lives and over a trillion dollars, it's time to do some nation-building right here at home.

You can choose a future where we reduce our deficit without wrecking our middle class. Independent analysis shows that my plan would cut our deficits by $4 trillion. Last summer, I worked with Republicans in Congress to cut $1 trillion in spending_ because those of us who believe government can be a force for good should work harder than anyone to reform it, so that it's leaner, more efficient, and more responsive to the American people.

I want to reform the tax code so that it's simple, fair, and asks the wealthiest households to pay higher taxes on incomes over $250,000_ the same rate we had when Bill Clinton was president; the same rate we had when our economy created nearly 23 million new jobs, the biggest surplus in history, and a lot of millionaires to boot.

Now, I'm still eager to reach an agreement based on the principles of my bipartisan debt commission. No party has a monopoly on wisdom. No democracy works without compromise. But when Gov. Romney and his allies in Congress tell us we can somehow lower our deficit by spending trillions more on new tax breaks for the wealthy_ well, you do the math. I refuse to go along with that. And as long as I'm president, I never will.

I refuse to ask middle class families to give up their deductions for owning a home or raising their kids just to pay for another millionaire's tax cut. I refuse to ask students to pay more for college; or kick children out of Head Start programs, or eliminate health insurance for millions of Americans who are poor, elderly, or disabled_ all so those with the most can pay less.

And I will never turn Medicare into a voucher. No American should ever have to spend their golden years at the mercy of insurance companies. They should retire with the care and dignity they have earned. Yes, we will reform and strengthen Medicare for the long haul, but we'll do it by reducing the cost of health care_ not by asking seniors to pay thousands of dollars more. And we will keep the promise of Social Security by taking the responsible steps to strengthen it_ not by turning it over to Wall Street.

This is the choice we now face. This is what the election comes down to. Over and over, we have been told by our opponents that bigger tax cuts and fewer regulations are the only way; that since government can't do everything, it should do almost nothing. If you can't afford health insurance, hope that you don't get sick. If a company releases toxic pollution into the air your children breathe, well, that's just the price of progress. If you can't afford to start a business or go to college, take my opponent's advice and "borrow money from your parents."

You know what? That's not who we are. That's not what this country's about. As Americans, we believe we are endowed by our creator with certain inalienable rights_ rights that no man or government can take away. We insist on personal responsibility and we celebrate individual initiative. We're not entitled to success. We have to earn it. We honor the strivers, the dreamers, the risk-takers who have always been the driving force behind our free enterprise system_ the greatest engine of growth and prosperity the world has ever known.

But we also believe in something called citizenship_ a word at the very heart of our founding, at the very essence of our democracy; the idea that this country only works when we accept certain obligations to one another, and to future generations.

We believe that when a CEO pays his autoworkers enough to buy the cars that they build, the whole company does better.

We believe that when a family can no longer be tricked into signing a mortgage they can't afford, that family is protected, but so is the value of other people's homes, and so is the entire economy.

We believe that a little girl who's offered an escape from poverty by a great teacher or a grant for college could become the founder of the next Google, or the scientist who cures cancer, or the President of the United States_ and it's in our power to give her that chance.

We know that churches and charities can often make more of a difference than a poverty program alone. We don't want handouts for people who refuse to help themselves, and we don't want bailouts for banks that break the rules. We don't think government can solve all our problems. But we don't think that government is the source of all our problems_ any more than are welfare recipients, or corporations, or unions, or immigrants, or gays, or any other group we're told to blame for our troubles.

Because we understand that this democracy is ours.

We, the people, recognize that we have responsibilities as well as rights; that our destinies are bound together; that a freedom which only asks what's in it for me, a freedom without a commitment to others, a freedom without love or charity or duty or patriotism, is unworthy of our founding ideals, and those who died in their defense.

As citizens, we understand that America is not about what can be done for us. It's about what can be done by us, together, through the hard and frustrating but necessary work of self-government.

So you see, the election four years ago wasn't about me. It was about you. My fellow citizens_ you were the change.

You're the reason there's a little girl with a heart disorder in Phoenix who'll get the surgery she needs because an insurance company can't limit her coverage. You did that.

You're the reason a young man in Colorado who never thought he'd be able to afford his dream of earning a medical degree is about to get that chance. You made that possible.

You're the reason a young immigrant who grew up here and went to school here and pledged allegiance to our flag will no longer be deported from the only country she's ever called home; why selfless soldiers won't be kicked out of the military because of who they are or who they love; why thousands of families have finally been able to say to the loved ones who served us so bravely: "Welcome home."

If you turn away now_ if you buy into the cynicism that the change we fought for isn't possible. well, change will not happen. If you give up on the idea that your voice can make a difference, then other voices will fill the void: lobbyists and special interests; the people with the $10 million checks who are trying to buy this election and those who are making it harder for you to vote; Washington politicians who want to decide who you can marry, or control health care choices that women should make for themselves.

Only you can make sure that doesn't happen. Only you have the power to move us forward.

I recognize that times have changed since I first spoke to this convention. The times have changed_ and so have I.

I'm no longer just a candidate. I'm the president. I know what it means to send young Americans into battle, for I have held in my arms the mothers and fathers of those who didn't return. I've shared the pain of families who've lost their homes, and the frustration of workers who've lost their jobs. If the critics are right that I've made all my decisions based on polls, then I must not be very good at reading them. And while I'm proud of what we've achieved together, I'm far more mindful of my own failings, knowing exactly what Lincoln meant when he said, "I have been driven to my knees many times by the overwhelming conviction that I had no place else to go."

But as I stand here tonight, I have never been more hopeful about America. Not because I think I have all the answers. Not because I'm nave about the magnitude of our challenges.

I'm hopeful because of you.

The young woman I met at a science fair who won national recognition for her biology research while living with her family at a homeless shelter_ she gives me hope.

The auto worker who won the lottery after his plant almost closed, but kept coming to work every day, and bought flags for his whole town and one of the cars that he built to surprise his wife_ he gives me hope.

The family business in Warroad, Minn., that didn't lay off a single one of their four thousand employees during this recession, even when their competitors shut down dozens of plants, even when it meant the owners gave up some perks and pay_ because they understood their biggest asset was the community and the workers who helped build that business_ they give me hope.

And I think about the young sailor I met at Walter Reed hospital, still recovering from a grenade attack that would cause him to have his leg amputated above the knee. Six months ago, I would watch him walk into a White House dinner honoring those who served in Iraq, tall and 20 pounds heavier, dashing in his uniform, with a big grin on his face; sturdy on his new leg. And I remember how a few months after that I would watch him on a bicycle, racing with his fellow wounded warriors on a sparkling spring day, inspiring other heroes who had just begun the hard path he had traveled.

He gives me hope.

I don't know what party these men and women belong to. I don't know if they'll vote for me. But I know that their spirit defines us. They remind me, in the words of scripture, that ours is a "future filled with hope."

And if you share that faith with me_ if you share that hope with me_ I ask you tonight for your vote.

If you reject the notion that this nation's promise is reserved for the few, your voice must be heard in this election.

If you reject the notion that our government is forever beholden to the highest bidder, you need to stand up in this election.

If you believe that new plants and factories can dot our landscape; that new energy can power our future; that new schools can provide ladders of opportunity to this nation of dreamers; if you believe in a country where everyone gets a fair shot, and everyone does their fair share, and everyone plays by the same rules, then I need you to vote this November.

America, I never said this journey would be easy, and I won't promise that now. Yes, our path is harder_ but it leads to a better place. Yes our road is longer_ but we travel it together. We don't turn back. We leave no one behind. We pull each other up. We draw strength from our victories, and we learn from our mistakes, but we keep our eyes fixed on that distant horizon, knowing that providence is with us, and that we are surely blessed to be citizens of the greatest nation on earth.

Thank you, God bless you, and may God bless these United States.

In his Speech he lays out everything we need to do in order to move the country ahead. Look at the Republican agenda and they want to take us back to the Failed Policies of Trickle Down Economics that the Bush Administration used to run this country in the Ditch. Tax Breaks for the Rich and Deregulate everything and you will be better off, that is called Austerity and we all saw how well that worked.

America at a Crossroads

We have reached a point in our history where there is no turning back. Let me explain. What we have seen for the last thirty years is a slow takeover from the Right Wing in this country. Most of us have been way to busy with all the day to day things we do as a family but for once we need to stop and look. If the Republicans win in November this country is lost as a Democracy and will become a Fascist Authoritarian government that will be fighting Wars all around the Planet, suppressing its own people, freedom will not exist as we have known it.

I will start with the Supreme Court. All the horrible things to obstruct from the Republicans have been about the control of the Supreme Court and installing a even more Right Wing Court that will strip all freedom from the People that they are suppose to defend.

Being a senior the next thing we need to talk about is Social Security.
No matter how the Republicans try to spin this they have one thing in mine and that is the hand over the Social Security reserve funds about 2.7 trillion dollars to Wall Street then cut off any new funds going into the funds until money is gone. We have seen just how honest Wall Street is. Even if Obama, is re-elected this will be a battle we as seniors will have to fight because Wall Street wants our

money and control so they can charge us fees and take bonuses off our hard earned Social Security Insurance payments from all our working lives.

On to Medicare, the Ryan Bill wants to create a Voucher System for this and actually they are lying about that. If you study the Ryan Bill you will see that they have made sure that Medicare will go broke right around 2016. Again they will tell you Good Luck, millions of seniors will be left to die in the streets.

Medicaid, here we go again in the Ryan Bill you will see they are going to slash 30% of the Budget. For those who do not grasp this it means that all those in Nursing Homes and the sickest and poorest people in this country will be left out in the Streets. Spin it all you want but that is the bottom line.

Education, again you must understand they have been working on this for 30 years to dumb down America. They love to take over state governments, then the first thing they do is slash the funds for schools, again the bottom line schools fail because they are not given the resources to succeed. Then the Republicans say with glee "SEE PUBLIC EDUCATION has failed" and we need to privatize. Once they have done that you will see every brainwashing tool ever invented tossed at our kids to make them only see the Right Wing Ideology.

FDA, backed by such giants as Monsanto, they want to end all regulations opening a new world, where they can poison us with unsafe foods and drugs. So much of this is already going on. This Department needs to be gutted of all the corporate insiders installed by the Bush Administration and even some by the Obama Administration. Must get stronger not ended.

EPA, backed by the Koch Brothers, you see the devil talking about ending all regulations on what we do with our water, air and all environmental issues. Fracking will be the Republican swan song about HOW WONDERFUL it is as they kill off our kids and grandkids with polluted air and water. We need to go to solar and wind and green technologies and Republicans will never allow us to escape the Fossil Fuel world of BIG OIL.

Women Issues, never have we seen such a all out attack on women as we have seen over the last two years once the Republicans took control of the House and so many State Governments, folks this is just the beginning soon they will be going after every single one of us.

Remember the LIE that got them elected to these offices, "JOBS JOBS JOBS" what are we hearing now from ROMNEY, the same bullshit that they gave us in 2010.

War, all you have to do is see who Romney has selected to head up his state department and you know right off WAR is all they want and will do. Romney, has even said he looks forward to the day he can attack IRAN and so the world what a great Commander in Chief he is. Sound Familiar, he is BUSH coming back to haunt us.

"One last thing, why does a Party need to Lie, set up Voter Suppression Laws, commit Election Fraud, fix computers to flip votes and bully people that come to vote? Maybe it is because this party has nothing good to offer the American People."
Jeff Carlson

Yes we have reached a crossroads, and we must for the sake of our families and country vote every single Republican out of office and send this Fascist Party back to be rebuilt by people that want to be part of America not rule it with a iron fist.

CROSSROADS MY VISION:

There are so many things that need to be done to take this country in a right direction and it all starts at the local level, meaning you, meaning me, meaning we all have a stake in it.

Lets start in your local area, if you have kids or even if you do not, you need to make sure they are getting the right support and curriculum for their schools. You might join the PTA, you just might volunteer to be a aid at your kids schools. It is a small step but you just might enjoy it and take it to the next level. School Boards, maybe even town council. When the Republicans decided to take over this country many decades ago, they put many boots on the ground at the local level and now dominate most of all those positions I mentioned above.

Now working to the state level much needs to done for even in the world of Democrats we do not have enough progressive candidates to make sure we get the things that need to be accomplished completed.

What to do? Not for all of us but we need many people, both young and old to get involved with the local and state politics. Maybe just volunteer to see if is for you. Join with all of us on the Social Media and get a feel for what the state and country need.

My wish list at the state level is that every state adopt a STATE BANK. this is going to be necessary to start pecking away at the powers of Wall Street.

Any State, that has RIGHT to WORK, VOTER ID and other ALEC written bills, needs to be looked at and reversed. That is why each and every state is important and each and every state has their own issues to be work on.

Again as I mentioned before the Republican strategy has always been start at local level then move to state level then take over the country. That way many do not know they are being strip of democracy until it is to late to reverse it out.

Once again this is not a overnight fix but a goal for a Progressive Government where we all share in the wealth, the education of our children, the protection of the environment and the growth as a "We the People" country.

Now at the federal level much needs to be done.

One, and this is a big one, we need to END Citizen United sooner than later. This Right Wing disaster was the worst Supreme Court ruling in my lifetime. It will take much work at the State level to get this accomplished but we must prevail to save what Democracy we have left.

So many people do not understand, this Ruling has opened the door for Corporations to BUY and OWN our Government. Need I say more they already own the Republican Party and are working hard to take over and buy the Democratic Party.

Now we know about Citizen United but we still have some options to at least slow down the effect of this bill. What that means is Congress needs to pass a FULL DISCLOSURE bill that will spell out Who is Funding what Super Packs.

So much money is now coming from other places than America to buy our elections and Politicians. This is against the constitution of America. But the U.S. Chamber of Commerce seems to think they do not need to follow the Constitution and are the leading bad guy with filtering money from overseas into the Super Packs. By the Way it is a great reason to get rid of all the Republicans, for they have blocked all attempts at getting this done.

The next one I am going to talk about is Student Loans and in earlier chapter I laid out just how we can eliminate all the Student Loans. Wall Street stole 14 trillion dollars from the American People and now it is time we collect at least something. The Five largest Banks will each be charged 1/5 of the amount of the student loans outstanding in this country. It would be a trillion dollar stimulus and would lead to much growth and buying power for those who actually drive the economy the working people we call consumers. The Republicans are again looking at Austerity that is nothing more than the Rich Stealing what is now left for the workers.

Then from that day forward Wall Street would be charged a processing fee of .005 on all transactions made each and everyday. This would generate enough money to fund all new students going to school forever. Education is the KEY to the Future and it means Education without ending up in Debt to Corporations to the day you die.

Now there is NO FREE LUNCH those receiving the funds would have to pay it back in some sort of service to the country. Peace Corps, Military, or many other functions that would help America Move Forward. This is being done in many countries around the world right now.

On my list that must be done: Energy a real strategy for the future. We are destroying the Planet with the idiotic quest to continue Fossil Fuels. We must DEMAND we change over to green technologies, the only way this is going to happen is get Democrats running the Congress.

Then we must hold their feet to the Fire using the Social Media to make sure we do as Germany just did, from 2000 to now, switched to WIND and SOLAR and ended their dependency on Fossil Fuel. This can be done but not if the Republicans control the Congress.
We all know that voting is the most important thing we can do as citizens so why do we not have our voting machines controlled by the government instead of private firms.
Can you imagine we have no idea about the software that controls them. This is a must fix or we will never be able to believe in elections again.

It blows me a way that the Romney Family controls the voting machines, in many of the key states in this election. How can anyone think this election will be fair. Only if Obama overcomes all the cheating from the Republicans and wins can we breathe easy.

Even if Obama wins we need to make it a priority of all progressives to change the way we vote. On that note we need to change the way elections are financed. Citizen United has forever changed politics in America and not for the good only for the greedy. What so many people do not know is money from all over the world is rolling into our election process and that is a disaster for democracy.

This was only my short list of many things that need to be done but everything I have listed can and must be done.

"We can and will again make America the greatest country in the world. It all starts with you and "WE THE PEOPLE" so much better sounding than that of "Hail the Corporation" that Republican Party represents."
Jeff Carlson

Epilogue

There are so many things that remain to be done in this country. President Barrack Obama has done a remarkable job to this point. He accomplished many things despite working with a Republican Party that has done nothing but conspire against him and the American people all in the hope that the people blame the President.

President Obama, deserves another 4 years so we may move the country forward. We all need to get out and vote because we know there will be many attempts by the Republicans to alter the votes and actually stop people from voting.

"Vote in numbers never seen in any election and the power of the people will overcome the greed of the Corporations."
Jeff Carlson

I hope you all enjoyed the book and you can see I love quotes, history and information that you can use over and over.
Now one more time let me take you to a place where you can use your imagination.

For me, I have this image in my head about stepping out on a podium and facing the world with my mom and dad right there where I can see them listening to me. The words I hear are those of Martin Luther King. With a strong voice my words flow:

I see a world where there is no War
I see a world where no children go hungry
I see a world where all people treat each other with respect

Then I close my eyes and I can hear John Lennon singing:

Imagine there's no heaven
It's easy if you try
No hell below us
Above us only sky
Imagine all the people living for today

Imagine there's no countries
It isn't hard to do
Nothing to kill or die for
And no religion too

Imagine all the people living life in peace

You, you may say
I'm a dreamer, but I'm not the only one
I hope some day you'll join us
And the world will be as one

Imagine no possessions
I wonder if you can
No need for greed or hunger
A brotherhood of man
Imagine all the people sharing all the world

You, you may say
I'm a dreamer, but I'm not the only one
I hope some day you'll join us
And the world will live as one

I have saved my favorite quote for last and I hope you enjoy.
"There are those who look at things the way they are, and ask why... I dream of things that never were, and ask why not?"
 Robert Francis Kennedy quotes (1925-1968)

There is something about Imagination that gives light and hope for the future of our country and our Planet.

"In our hands we hold the destiny to our country to our environment for our families and to the well being of all creatures on this planet. There are times in history where, 'We the People', need to come together and do the right thing, this is one of those times"
Jeff Carlson

Made in the USA
Charleston, SC
06 August 2013